Anarchism After Deleuze and Guattari

Deleuze and Guattari Encounters

Series Editor: Ian Buchanan, Director of the Institute for Social Transformation Research, University of Wollongong, Australia

Titles available in the series:

Cinema After Deleuze
Richard Rushton

Philosophy After Deleuze
Joe Hughes

Political Theory After Deleuze
Nathan Widder

Theology After Deleuze
Kristien Justaert

Music After Deleuze
Edward Campbell

Space After Deleuze
Arun Saldanha

Anarchism After Deleuze and Guattari
Chantelle Gray

Anarchism After Deleuze and Guattari

Fabulating Futures

Chantelle Gray

BLOOMSBURY ACADEMIC
LONDON • NEW YORK • OXFORD • NEW DELHI • SYDNEY

BLOOMSBURY ACADEMIC
Bloomsbury Publishing Plc
50 Bedford Square, London, WC1B 3DP, UK
1385 Broadway, New York, NY 10018, USA
29 Earlsfort Terrace, Dublin 2, Ireland

BLOOMSBURY, BLOOMSBURY ACADEMIC and the Diana logo are
trademarks of Bloomsbury Publishing Plc

First published in Great Britain 2022
This paperback edition published 2024

Cover design by Charlotte Daniels
Cover image: Italian Anarchist female fighter in Madrid, Batallon de la Muerte September 24,
1936. (© Sueddeutsche Zeitung Photo / Alamy)

A catalogue record for this book is available from the British Library.

A catalog record for this book is available from the Library of Congress.

ISBN: HB: 978-1-3501-3239-9
          PB: 978-1-3503-3491-5
        ePDF: 978-1-3501-3240-5
       eBook: 978-1-3501-3241-2

Series: Deleuze and Guattari Encounters

Typeset by Integra Software Services Pvt. Ltd.

To find out more about our authors and books visit www.bloomsbury.com
and sign up for our newsletters.

To Aragorn, and Britta

Contents

List of figures   viii

Acknowledgements   ix

List of abbreviations   x

Introduction: The Deleuze-Guattari-anarchism machine   1

1   Statist realism   11

2   Axiomatics of the State   33

3   Capital: A nervous condition   57

4   Hacking for our lives   77

5   To believe in this world again   101

6   Constructing the revolution   125

Lines of leakage: The black flag, for life   149

Notes   153

Bibliography   160

Index   174

Figures

1 Bernie Sanders/Subcomandante Marcos image.
   Courtesy of Carla Saunders and Anastasya Eliseeva   12

Acknowledgements

Heartfelt thanks to Aragorn Eloff, Jesse Cohn, Delphi Carstens, Evelien Geertz, Anné Verhoef and Joff Bradley for reading parts, or all, of the manuscript and providing me with invaluable comments and advice. I would also like to say a very special thank you to the two blind peer reviewers who offered thoughtful feedback for incorporation. To Carla Saunders and Anastasya Eliseeva, my gratitude for helping me render the Bernie Sanders/Subcomandante Marcos image. I am grateful to Ian Buchanan for encouraging me to take up the project but, more importantly, for camaraderie and academic generosity. My appreciation goes out to Jade Grogan, Suzie Nash and the Bloomsbury team for all their hard work. To my friends who supported me through this project, and to the School of Philosophy at North-West University, three cheers! Finally, to the many scholars and anarchists who have shaped my thoughts and actions over the years, I am deeply appreciative.

Abbreviations

Abbreviations of works by Deleuze (including those written with Guattari and Parnet) and Guattari (including those written with Suely Rolnik)

AO   *Anti-Oedipus: Capitalism and Schizophrenia Vol. 1*

AOP   *The Anti-Oedipus Papers*

ATP   *A Thousand Plateaus: Capitalism and Schizophrenia Vol. 2*

B   *Bergsonism*

C2   *Cinema 2: The Time-Image*

CH   *Chaosmosis: An Ethico-aesthetic Paradigm*

D   *Dialogues*

DI   *Desert Islands and Other Texts 1953–1974*

DR   *Difference and Repetition*

E   *Expressionism in Philosophy: Spinoza*

F   *Foucault*

H   *Empiricism and Subjectivity: An Essay on Hume's Theory of Human Nature*

K   *Kafka: Toward a Minor Literature (1986)*

L   *The Fold: Leibniz and the Baroque*

LF   *Lines of Flight: For Another World of Possibilities*

LS   *The Logic of Sense*

M	*Masochism: Coldness and Cruelty*
MRB	*Molecular Revolution in Brazil*
N	*Negotiations, 1972–1990*
P	*Proust and Signs*
PP	*Spinoza: Practical Philosophy*
PT	*Psychoanalysis and Transversality: Texts and Interviews 1955–1971*
SS	*Soft Subversions: Text and Interviews 1977–1985*
TE	*The Three Ecologies*
TR	*Two Regimes of Madness, Texts and Interviews 1975–1995*
WP	*What Is Philosophy?*

Introduction: The Deleuze-Guattari-anarchism machine

I discovered anarchism at the same time I discovered Deleuze and Guattari. It was a rupture, to say the least. Everything I thought I knew became a question, a questioning – an encounter with that which exceeded all signification. I found myself an apprentice with a task: learn to believe in *this* world. In truth, I became an apprentice of Nietzsche's paradox, as I like to think Deleuze was, wondering what I would do if 'some day or night a demon were to steal' after me into my loneliest loneliness and say to me I had to live the life I have lived 'once more and innumerable times' (Nietzsche 1974: 273). Would I throw myself down on the floor and, gnashing my teeth, curse the demon? Or would I boldly answer: 'You are a god and never have I heard anything more divine' (Nietzsche 1974: 273). I do not have an answer to this question yet. I remain an apprentice, but I have learnt *so much* from Deleuze, Guattari and hundreds of anarchists about the importance of continuing the struggle to destroy the many intersecting lines of domination – in the world as much as in my own thoughts; the value of community, the value of care – of caring for the people we are and can become, of caring for the world and finding reasons to believe in it, despite abundant reasons not to.

And there are abundant reasons not to. Climate collapse and everything that it augurs – drought, food insecurity, water scarcity, loss of biodiversity, loss of oxygen, loss of life. Wars, armed conflicts, states of exception, states of emergency. Naturalized forms of State oppression, racism, patriarchy, wealth disparity (capitalism), class inequalities and nationalism (to name only a few of the molar determinations). The encroachment of algorithmic reason into every aspect of life (one needs simply to think here of Mark Zuckerberg's metaverse). Not to mention broken social relations, the proliferation of conspiracy theories and fake news, election hacking, large-scale right-wing mobilization, disease and pandemics. (As I write this book, the Covid-19 pandemic is about to enter its third year. We have lost so much already.) It would seem, then, that devastation is the 'new normal', so part of our everyday lives that it has been all but invisibilized. Given this, why should we bother finding reasons to believe in this world? Why should we bother trying to change anything? And why on earth should we bother with anarchism?

We do it, as Uri Gordon says, for its own sake. We experiment with 'non-hierarchical, voluntary, cooperative, solidaric and playful' ways of living and being for *their own sake*, because we believe it is worthwhile for that reason. After all, the task for anarchists 'is not to "introduce" a new society but to realize it as much as possible in the present tense' (2007: 46). The reward is freedom, and a memory of freedom – for the yet-to-come, the people-to-come. As Franco 'Bifo' Berardi puts it:

> My knowledge and understanding miss the event, the singularity. So I must act 'as if'. As if the forces of labor and knowledge might overcome the forces of greed and of proprietary obsession. As if the cognitive workers might overcome the fractalization of their life and intelligence, and give birth to the self-organization of collective knowledge. I must resist simply because I cannot know what will happen after the future, and I must preserve the consciousness and sensibility of social solidarity, of human empathy, of gratuitous activity – of freedom, equality, and fraternity. Just in case, right? Just because we don't know what is going to happen next, in the empty space that comes after the future of modernity. (Berardi 2011: 163)

To be sure, believing in this world is a gratuitous activity, but one we cannot afford to negate for our very lives – the lives of all inhabitants of this planet – depend on it. The stakes are huge, and we may already be too late. But we have to act *as if*. As if we have to live *this* life in *this* world once more and innumerable times. That is the challenge. That is the apprenticeship.

In bringing together Deleuze, Guattari and anarchism, I hope to respond to this challenge in some small way, though I must confess that bringing together these large bodies of work in an introductory text was itself a challenge. I have, for example, not said nearly enough about climate change – not for lack of interest, but because this warrants a book-length project of its own. For the same reason I have not said nearly enough about colonialism, race, patriarchy or gender more broadly, though I have tried to include multiple voices and stories that cover these important issues. In the end, I brought together what resonated most strongly for me in these diverse bodies of work, while also aiming to give readers an anarchism they can believe in – as one reader prompted me early on to do. Given this, it is my sincere hope that this little book disturbs the slumber of thought, even in the most miniscule of ways, and sparks reasons to believe in this world. In the words of Deleuze: 'Whether we are Christians or atheists, in our universal schizophrenia, we need reasons to believe in this world' (C2: 172).

Following the method used by Deleuze and Guattari in *Anti-Oedipus*, the book is divided into two parts or, to be more precise, two movements, like musical movements, consisting of different speeds that make the whole proliferate in a generalized chromaticism – placing 'elements of any nature in continuous variation' in an attempt to 'give rise to new distinctions' while not expecting any particular outcome in advance, nor taking any 'as final' (*ATP* 97). The first part of this book, then, is a critical-clinical project, aimed at uncovering *why* it is difficult to think beyond the State and capitalism; diagnosing *how* the State constructs statist realism and so perpetuates its dogmatic image of thought in society, and understanding how capitalism multiplies forms of alienation. These are questions that have been grappled with by anarchists as much as by Deleuze and Guattari, often drawing on the same resources, such as the anthropological work of Pierre Clastres who was, in fact, an anarchist and whose work – like that of other anarchist and anarchistic anthropologists such as David Graeber and James C. Scott – has shown that, in contrast to ideas perpetuated by the likes of Thomas Hobbes, the State neither saved people from 'survival in a dog-eat-dog world', nor was it *at any point* 'the result of a consensual process designed to protect people's liberties and well-being' (Gelderloos 2016: 3). The State was neither necessary nor inevitable; it was, rather, as studies by Clastres, Graeber and Scott show, a contested social form that emerged from contingent conditions. This is what Deleuze and Guattari mean when they say the State 'comes into the world fully formed and rises up in a single stroke' (*ATP* 427).

Similarly, in thinking about capitalism, we see that Deleuze and Guattari's analysis is closer to anarchist analyses than Marxist analyses because the problem for them is not so much about needs-based production versus alienated labour as it is about what capitalism has done to processes of subjectivation and by what means such capitalist modes of living have become normalized. Deleuze and Guattari, like anarchists, emphasize the delirium of the capitalist system, observing that it is precisely its irrationality that makes it work well. Capitalism, after all, thrives on chaos, crises and change, transforming and updating itself continuously, mobilizing mutations and deterritorialized flows by recuperating them for its own ends. Yet despite these resonances, Deleuze and Guattari never credit anarchists and seemingly make no real effort to engage with the history and theory of anarchism. To boot, the terms 'anarchism' and 'anarchy' are used inconsistently in their individual and collective oeuvres, sometimes positively and sometimes negatively. So why bring together Deleuze, Guattari and anarchism? And why call the book *Anarchism After Deleuze and Guattari*? Deleuze and Guattari were, ultimately, not part of any anarchist movements and anarchism developed *before* they started theorizing.

The simple answer is that this is the convention of the book series: *[Subject] After Deleuze and Guattari*. And true enough, Deleuze and Guattari have inflected anarchist theory and praxis in recent years, evidenced by a number of books such as *The Political Philosophy of Poststructuralist Anarchism* (1994) by Todd May; *The Politics of Postanarchism* (2010) by Saul Newman; *Returning to Revolution: Deleuze, Guattari and Zapatismo* (2012) by Thomas Nail; *Anarchism and Political Modernity* (2012) by Nathan Jun; and *Deleuze and Anarchism* (2019) by Chantelle Gray van Heerden and Aragorn Eloff. By the same token, Deleuze and Guattari's philosophy was inflected by anarchism, even if only obliquely so through, for example, their encounter with Clastres. Perhaps a better way of thinking about the book, then, is anarchism *and* Deleuze *and* Guattari because rather than attempting to *post hoc* label Deleuze and Guattari anarchists, it tries to show that bringing together anarchism and Deleuze and Guattari is productive for outlining a symptomatology of the effects of the State apparatus and capitalism, and thinking, for example, of how the State instills a unity of composition via its axiomatic presuppositions which provide it with a certain amount of uniformity despite its historically variable forms. Thinking, too, about how its power of appropriation works – which does not refer only to its capacities to capture identities, land, natural resources, thoughts and ways of life, but also to the way in which it appropriates or coopts anticipation-prevention mechanisms. Uncovering these logics, of which statist axioms form a part, is vital because it denaturalizes the idea that the State is necessary and inevitable, as well as the notion that the State form is the best or most progressive structure for socio-political organization which, in turn, unshackles thought from the constraints of what I call statist realism.

Bringing together Guattari and anarchism and Deleuze is, moreover, useful for describing what is emerging rather than simply what is established the new forms of governmentality arresting our thoughts, our ways of living and the unfolding of the future. As McKenzie Wark reminds us, it is *our task* to describe what is emerging rather than what is established. Is this not, after all, what made the work of Marx, anarchists and Deleuze and Guattari revolutionary? If, however, 'one starts with what is established, it is easy to interpret any new aspect' of the emerging context 'as simply variations on the same essence. Starting with what may be emerging', on the other hand, 'provides a suitable derangement of the senses, a giddy hint that all that was solid is melting into air' (Wark 2019: 42). To this end, Chapter 4 is devoted to grappling with the digital milieu and its ethicopolitical arrangements of assumptions and propositions about the world, as well as some of the effects these are having on society. Many theorists and practitioners – including philosophers, psychologists, media studies researchers, qualitative sociologists, anthropologists and medical science researchers – have, over the past decade or so, critiqued the wide deployment of algorithms and other automated processes on epistemological, political, legal and ethical grounds. The fascination and antipathy have, in part, to do with the abstrusity of algorithmic logics and architecture for public scrutiny (see, for example, Pasquale 2015; Burrell 2016; Noble 2018). Two obvious problems are thus transparency and accountability, though this chapter looks beyond issues of reform to grapple, instead, with the effects of digitization on inter- and transgenerational memory and practices that provide consistency through social inscription from one generation to the next. Here I bring Guattari, Deleuze and anarchism in conversation with Bernard Stiegler's work because he most consistently wrestles in his work with these questions, aiming always to understand whether 'the development of artificial intelligence and machine learning' will 'allow us to rejoin life' or not (Yuk Hui in Lovink 2019). To state it somewhat differently, Stiegler argues that technology is always a *pharmakon* – both a poison and a cure. What determines which of these immanent conditions becomes amplified depends on our attention to and care of it.

This is important for political philosophy because, as Dan McQuillan argues, the shift to AI governmentality 'can be understood as an upgrade to the existing bureaucratic order' (2020), meaning it is part and parcel of what Scott calls the 'social engineering' practices of the State (1998: 183). Specifically, it speaks to the problem of legibility which not only ensures resonance between disparate societal spheres but also political surveillance since it renders space manageable and human action predictable through subjectification processes. These, in turn, engender patterned behaviours and thoughts that are now externally managed vis-à-vis algorithms which have come to replace earlier reward-punishment mechanisms. But it also speaks to risk management, futures markets and derivatives which ensure continued social stratification and debt – both monetary and 'a debt that is the inverse of "social credit", an algorithmic negative that cuts off access to societies' (McQuillan 2020). Equally, our technological innovations are challenging ecological boundaries in unprecedented ways, so we need new paradigms for thinking through these unique challenges. Useful here is diffracting Murray Bookchin's theory of *social ecology* with Guattari's work on ecosophy as both see the ecological and social crises implicated in mental ecology. Social ecology, like ecosophy, is thus a holistic response that 'challenges the entire system of domination itself and seeks to eliminate the hierarchical and class edifice that has imposed itself on humanity and defined the relationship between nonhuman and human nature' (Bookchin 1993). I further their work by implicating them in algorithmic ecology because, as Deleuze and Guattari remind us, we cannot separate out the natural from the machinic. Algorithms are not just simple passive technological extensions of our capacities, but fellow inhabitants of our machinic phylum.

The final two chapters constitute the positive project, a praxis 'animated by an insurrectionary desire, a utopian energy and a fundamental rejection of political authority' (Newman 2010a: 17). Having outlined, clearly, the 'rejection of capitalism, imperialism and feudalism; all trade agreements, institutions and governments that promote destructive globalization'; 'all forms and systems of domination and discrimination including, but not limited to, patriarchy, racism and religious fundamentalism of all creeds', these chapters map some of the ways in which we can 'embrace the full dignity of all' beings – human, nonhuman and more-than-human alike (Gordon 2007: 35). Diffusing the work of Deleuze and Guattari through anarchism and vice versa, I link practices like prefiguration to *care* and *careful* experimentation, to *taking care of* life and the living through emergent strategies that can 'sustain our relationships and collective visions, uphold our values', 'break cycles of harm' and help us create healthy movements through which we refuse to cancel us (brown 2020: 6, 7). We are, after all, 'seeding the future' with 'every action we take' – 'our smallest choices today will become our next norms' (brown 2020: 2). So we must act *as if*, not for profit, but for freedom. To this end, the positive project is aimed at creating a feeling that life is worth living for the benefit of a time yet-to-come and a people yet-to-come, but in the here and now by reinvigorating our practices, prefiguring revolutionary conditions and fabulating new forms of subjectivity.

Although primarily aimed at Deleuzoguattarian scholars and anarchists, it is my hope that this book will be read by a broader audience. As such, I have tried to render the specialist language of the theorists I have used into more accessible language without dumbing down the ideas contained therein. Whether I have been successful remains to be seen. What I wanted to give readers is not only a broad scope of the overlaps between anarchism, Deleuze and Guattari, but also new theories for taking forward our practices into the future in continuous variation and as active experimentations. This entails 'paying attention to discomforting as well as joyous affective and material relations' and ushering in 'new sensorial, affective domains of possibility – which will mean paying attention to (and not turning away from) "sad" passions (such as paranoia, depression, schizophrenia, etc.)' (Geerts and Carstens 2019: 920). Perhaps this is why Deleuze and Guattari argue that believing in this world is our most difficult task – because it entails affirming *all of chance* and, from that, fabulating a mode of existence that simultaneously requires an ability to attentively carve some consistency out of the 'chaos' that any new situation presents *and* continuing experimentation for the creation of novel relations. This, moreover, by means of 'immanent modes of existence' rather than 'recourse to transcendent values' (*E* 269). As Deleuze reminds us: 'The question is in each case: Does, say, this feeling, increase our power of action or not? Does it help us come into full possession of that power? To do all we can is our ethical task properly so called' (*E* 269). *Our ethical task properly so called: diagnosing the symptoms of society, formulating or posing problems at the level of practice, and fabulating more therapeutic ways of living that renew and conserve our being, that renew and conserve the world.*

Clandestine passengers on a motionless voyage, welcome to the apprenticeship.

Statist realism

Cast your mind back to 20 January 2021, an auspicious day marking the end of the Trump era and the dawn of sanity. Or so much of the world keeps hoping. Remarkable about this day was not the inauguration of Joe Biden as the forty-sixth US president, but the virulent meme of Vermont Senator Bernie Sanders, a maddening reminder of what could have been – twice! Recall that, in 2016, Sanders sought the Democratic Party's vote but lost to former Secretary of State, Hillary Clinton, at the New York primary. Sanders ran again for the presidential candidacy in 2020 but dropped out on 8 April to support Joe Biden and unite against Donald Trump. In a live-streamed speech, Sanders explained: 'In this most desperate hour, I cannot in good conscience continue to mount a campaign that cannot win and which would interfere with the important work required of all of us … While this campaign is coming to an end, our movement is not' (Ember 2020). The withdrawal notwithstanding, it was Sanders who stole the spotlight at Biden's inauguration when a photograph – taken on the day by Washington-based photojournalist, Brendan Smialowski – went viral. Unremarkable in most ways, the image features Sen. Sanders sitting cross-legged on a chair, donning knitted wool mittens, a sensible winter coat and a mask, the latter a crude mnemonic of the ongoing Covid-19 pandemic. Pedestrian indeed, yet something of the mood in this quotidian photo captured the imagination of the world. What began as a Twitter post by Ashley Smalls soon snowballed into an internet sensation, with Sanders transposed into virtually every conceivable situation. Bernie as a Golden Girl, Bernie next to Forest

Figure 1 Bernie Sanders/Subcomandante Marcos image. Courtesy of Carla Saunders and Anastasya Eliseeva.

Gump, Bernie as baby Yoda, anime Bernie in *Totoro* and, in one of my favourite if more obscure images, Bernie next to a grand piano 'performing' John Cage's 4'33".

Beyond the facile interpretations of its curmudgeonly disposition, what captured the social imaginary was, in a bitter twist of irony, an acknowledgement of *the end of imagination*, as Arundhati Roy once named it; an appreciation that, despite running up against a limit, 'the stakes we're playing for are huge. Our fatigue and our shame could mean the end of us. The end of our children and our children's children. Of everything we love' (Roy 2016: 5). A placeholder, then, for the failure of imagination, for the failure to think outside the constraints of our limitations, counting the limitations of liberal or representative democracy, which, as Cindy Milstein points out, is a rather anachronistic ideal given that democracies comprise 'layers of nonrepresentative statecraft' that 'now work hand in hand with equally undemocratic international NGOs and multinational financial bodies' (2010: 35). In a very real sense, the Sanders meme represents the failure of imagination *and* the failure of the State, yet a world beyond the State is inconceivable to most human beings. This, in spite of the fact that we have only lived as statist societies for a relatively short period of our history. Moreover, Sanders's policies are all but radical. Murray Bookchin describes his notion of 'open government' as 'personal paternalism rather than democracy' – a form of socialism aimed at facilitating 'the ease with which business interests can profit from the city', as is evidenced by 'the extraordinary privileges Sanders has provided to the most predatory enterprises' (2016). Sanders, in other words, may be a socialist democrat, but he firmly supports a market economy – he merely proposes some regulation and reform. Granted, Sanders is certainly more likeable than Trump, at least in leftist circles, and he does have better politics on the whole, but they are not as progressive as many would like to believe. And yet, for lack of anything else, the Sanders meme became a placeholder for hope, albeit a twisted kind of hope, because contained within it lies a thought-provoking political paradox: on the one hand, the visceral relief at regime change, on the other, the concomitant collective 'meh' directed at the new commander in chief. This is what the late Mark Fisher called *reflexive impotence* – an apathetic cynicism according to which people recognize that something is wrong, at the same time conceding their own inability to change the situation, often because they *think* change is impossible. This inability to act provokes a 'passive observation' which 'forecloses any possibility of politicization', often leading to *depressive hedonia* – a pervasive sense that 'something is missing', that little matters beyond the pursuit of what often turns out to be empty pleasure – which, in turn, engenders numerous forms of *interpassivity*, a kind of outsourcing of activities, including politics (2009: 21, 22). Effectively, the Bernie meme 'performed' politics 'for' people because of an inescapable feeling that nothing anybody does can change anything, so why try to do something at all? We have run up against a limit: the end of imagination.

This is what I call *statist realism*,[1] riffing on Fisher's notion of *capitalist realism*, expounded in his 2009 book of the same name. Pivoting on the slogan attributed to both Frederic Jameson and Slavoj Žižek 'that it is easier to imagine the end of the world than it is to imagine the end of capitalism', Fisher argues that capitalism has infiltrated the social imaginary to the extent that it is now presumed, almost universally, to be the 'only viable political and economic system' – so much so, in fact, that it has become impossible for most people to contemplate a *feasible* alternative to it, especially given the failure of socialist experiments around the world (2009: 2). Like capitalist realism, statist realism goes hand in hand with the prevalent 'sense of exhaustion, of cultural and political sterility' that forms the background conditioning of our collective thought and action (Fisher 2009: 7). Said in plain language, statist realism posits the State as the horizon of human possibility in such a manner that a *coherent* and *viable* replacement for it is virtually inconceivable. What we have, in effect, is an image of society – *doxa* – that overlays all other thought and so makes it impossible to think of life outside of or beyond statist societies. Deleuze calls this the 'dogmatic image of thought' or, with Guattari, 'statist thought' – when thought itself conforms to the *form* of the State apparatus: the arboreal, hierarchizing, homogenizing, normalizing and territorializing mechanism by which a social field is organized in statist societies. It is, in essence, the reproduction of the logics and techniques of the State in our thought patterns, and it is precisely this image of thought which limits our imagination and subsequent action because it *conditions* the field of possibility where thinking and action unfold. The State, as the horizon of human possibility, thus becomes the horizon of the *thinkable*.

In terms of capitalist realism, this is due to the subordination of oneself to a 'reality that is infinitely plastic, capable of reconfiguring itself at any moment' (Fisher 2009: 54) – an adaptive mode that short-circuits our ways of being and thinking, as we see in Chapters 4–6 – whereas statist realism denotes the cognitive-affective distribution of 'inevitabilism', a sense of incontrovertible certainty, a feeling that nothing can be changed outside of State politics. *It is our best hope even if it is an imperfect system.* The consequence is an inexorable repetition of the same – what Deleuze calls 'dead repetition' – because the world, and thought, has collapsed in on itself, producing a kind of Truman Show reality. Emancipatory politics, in contrast, as 'any number of radical theorists from Brecht through to Foucault and Badiou have maintained', entails on the one hand the destruction of 'the appearance of a "natural order"' and, on the other, the concomitant revelation that 'what is presented as necessary and inevitable' is 'a mere contingency, just as it must make what was previously deemed to be impossible seem attainable' (Fisher 2009: 17).

The dogmatic image of thought, or: The logics of statist realism

In *Difference and Repetition*, Deleuze outlines eight postulates of the image of thought to explain how something like statist realism works or, in more philosophical terms, how it is structured in thought and carried out in the world. The first postulate is twofold: the idea that thought is naturally virtuous and, following from this, the idea that people naturally seek out and express good-natured thought. Deleuze calls this 'good sense' (*DR* 132). The second postulate, which Deleuze describes as 'common sense', denotes a natural commonality or cohesion (universality, harmony) between the faculties of thought (*DR* 134). Together, the first two postulates constitute the two halves of *doxa*, often conveyed as something like *everybody knows, no one can deny*. The third postulate holds that once reality is apprehended and distributed between the faculties, thought is assimilated according to a formula of recognition rather than one which allows for wonder or 'surprise'. This formula of recognition functions by assimilating new experiences and incoming sensations according to resemblance, identity, analogy and opposition so that new information can be assigned a stable identity – this is how the multiplicity of difference becomes subordinated to the One of identity (*DR* 116–17). Meaning and value are now produced based on a presupposition of harmony between the faculties which are themselves thought to be identical (*DR* 133). The problem for Deleuze is that these presuppositions prevent anything from surprising us or causing a 'shock' to thought because new content always-already conforms to the form of the dogmatic image of thought. Under these conditions thought is constrained to what is already known because there is a conservative and regulative logic at work which inhibits radical cogitation; that is, thought conforms to a model or image that takes for granted certain criteria according to which all new sensations or experiences must be judged. Once novel information is matched with existing knowledge, a consistent representation of the world is formed, even when there is a mismatch between the world of representation and the world of presentation (the world as it is). The reason should be clear by now: the assimilating functions of thought have become overgeneralized, subordinating difference 'to the complementary dimensions of the Same and the Similar, the Analogous and the Opposed', as is explained in the fourth postulate (*DR* 167). In this way a closed loop is created so that existing knowledge cannot be questioned because 'everybody knows'. *Everybody knows the world would go up in flames without States.* The upshot of these kinds of thought pattern is that even when experience does not match our existing knowledge, the mismatch is often designated a failure of recognition – an empirical and external failure (*DR* 149) – rather than a failure of thought itself. This is how the dogmatic image of thought remains intact because we never get to question pre-existing knowledge; an error is never a productive break or gap between the faculties, or between experience and pre-existing knowledge, which would allow for an opening to the outside of the image of thought where genuinely novel thought can unfold.

The final three postulates are rather more philosophically technical. The sixth concerns the proposition itself, specifically the way in which the proposition of the dogmatic image of thought designates its form as the sole 'logical form of recognition' (*DR* 154). Accordingly, the dogmatic image of thought illegitimately elevates its empirical content to a transcendental form. In other words, the postulate designates itself as that from which new thought emerges when it in fact only conditions and constrains incoming experience, sensations and thought. For example, when a certain belief becomes widely accepted as correct, it becomes axiomatic or self-evident, which is to say a presupposition of reasoning. We will see in Chapter 2 how State violence is widely presumed to be secondary or necessary to keep 'civil order', when in fact it was originary. But, because it is widely assumed to be true or correct, the idea of State violence as secondary forms the basis for all ensuing thought about the State. This constrains thought to the circular logic of the State apparatus. Deleuze argues, in the seventh postulate, that this model of knowledge does not allow us to pose good questions or problems. That is, the questions or problems posed are not raised correctly or rigorously enough 'at the level of practice' (*H* 16, 107) and are, as a result, false problems because they pre-empt the types of solutions that are imaginable. And, as Deleuze reminds us, a 'solution always has the truth it deserves according to the problem to which it is a response, and the problem always has the solution it deserves in proportion to its own truth or falsity – in other words, in proportion to its sense' (*DR* 159). This is what the Bernie meme illustrates: instead of the failure of the State prompting questions about the suitability of the State form for organizing human social relations, its axiomatic or transcendental status merely generates questions around the content so that it becomes assumed that what is needed is a different president or political party rather than the reorganization of society itself. To think about how we actually discover new knowledge and how learning takes place Deleuze argues, in the final postulate, that thinking cannot be reduced to a mere 'training' of the mind which often takes place via standardized forms of knowledge production and its mechanical reproduction because this form of knowledge determines *in advance* what kinds of thought we are likely to have (*DR* 166).

All States, regardless of the form of government they take, 'need an image of thought' as their 'axiomatic system or abstract machine' which provides them with 'the strength to function' (*D* 88). That is to say, once an image of thought becomes adopted, distributed and normalized in society, it becomes invisibilized so that it 'naturally' translates into a style of life – even a collective style of life – that bolsters State aims. This image of thought is, moreover, resonated through other institutions in society – the family, the school, the military, the workplace. 'What one learns at school or in the university is not essentially a content or data, but a behavioral model adapted' (*SS* 11). Deleuze and Guattari would say that the image of thought has changed something fundamentally at the level of desire and that this new desire has become propagated throughout the social field. *We cannot think beyond State societies because we desire to live in societies that are organized and governed by the State.* The State, in other words, has become the limit not only of our imagination, but of what we want. Of what we desire. This may seem a rather radical stance to take, but the problem of desire was one of the greatest mysteries for Deleuze and Guattari – one which, for them, speaks directly to the problem of politics.

While not using the specialized language of Deleuze and Guattari, anarchist critiques of the State resonate with many of their analyses. In fact, its origins as a political theory and praxis – which stretch back to the end of the eighteenth century in Europe (though further back in more prefigural forms and before it was explicitly called 'anarchism') – can be seen as a response to the increased power of centralized States and their attendant strong nationalisms on the one hand, and widespread capitalism and industrialization, as well as their effects on society, on the other. Anti-statism and anti-capitalism are thus two of the core values of anarchism, though anarchist thought on the State – like any other category of analysis – is by no means homogenous, nor can anarchism be defined solely in terms of its opposition to the State, in some measure because this critique forms part of a broader theorization on hierarchy, domination – including patriarchy and race – power and authority and should, therefore, be understood as part of a constellation of concepts. Besides, many leftist groups are anti-statist; what 'differentiates anarchism from other ideologies' is not anti-statism per se, 'but the particular meanings and degrees of relative significance' given 'to concepts in relation to other concepts' – a process from which emerges a unique 'understanding of the nature and function of the state' (Jun 2019: 29). This is remarkably similar to Deleuze and Guattari's distinctive constellative approach which they use to formulate normative critiques of the State, its logics or abstract machines and its centres of power, as well as strategies for its dismantlement.

Anarchism in Europe[2] developed parallel to, and as a critique of, Marxism, even though it was the latter that would become more popular. An early anarchist, Pierre-Joseph Proudhon, in fact greatly influenced Marx and 'anticipated many Marxist arguments before they were ostensibly "invented" by' him (Shannon, Nocella II and Asimakopoulos 2012: 14). Because of the milieu from which it emerged, early European anarchism was imbued with ideas about liberty, justice and equality alongside critiques of capitalism and the State. Mikhail Bakunin, another contemporary of Marx, argued that the State constitutes a political abstraction that does not represent the 'positive and real interests' of the people it is supposed to govern and look after because it is, principally, an 'agent of exploitation', an apparatus that upholds the interests of only one class, the bourgeoisie (Bakunin 1977a: 82). Bakunin's critique here is not merely that the State does not represent the interests of people; he is critiquing the very idea of representation because representation, especially government representation, tends to be partial and separates people from their capacities to act directly and according to their own needs and desires. Representation is thus a mechanism by which statist images of thought are produced and according to which the State is reproduced. Bakunin also recognized that the State creates its own reasons for existence, so establishing 'itself as the supreme and absolute end' – a universal necessity (1977b: 140). This is one of the binding axioms, or dogmatic images of thought, of the State and is an idea that became normalized via Enlightenment thinkers like Thomas Hobbes, John Locke and David Hume, as we see in Chapter 2.

Like Bakunin, Peter Kropotkin also viewed the State as an abstraction, an unnecessary form of authoritarian organization that acts as an obstacle to social change (1970: 66, 211). Significantly, he recognized the contingency of the State form: 'The state is only one of the forms adopted by society in the course of history', he writes. 'Why then make no distinction between what is permanent and what is accidental?' (Kropotkin 1970: 212). Kropotkin, moreover, understood something about the capturing mechanisms and self-replicative capabilities of the State: 'Either the State will be destroyed and a new life will begin in thousands of centers ... or else the State must crush the individual and local life, it must become master of all domains of human activity, must bring with it wars and internal struggles for the possession of power' (Kropotkin 1943: 44). These ideas resonate strongly with Deleuze and Guattari's understanding of the State as contingent and as an apparatus of capture which provide important counterpoints to the notion of the State as necessary. It also reflects the idea that the State apparatus functions via centres of resonance, which is to say that the State form captures different power relations and centres through which it reproduces itself, including pedagogy, the economic sphere, the law, familial and sexual domains, and so on. This is what Kropotkin means when he says that the State crushes individual and local life: it encroaches on every sphere until it settles as a pervasive condition. It is for this reason that Gustav Landauer describes the State as a certain 'relationship between human beings, a way by which people relate to one another' and which causes us to behave differently to one another, thereby destroying certain kinds of relationality in favour of interactions that serve State ends (2005: 165). This critique is close to Foucault's ideas on governmentality and power, where governmentality is a mode of power that conducts the conduct of people, so structuring 'the possible field of action of others' (Foucault 2000: 341). Echoing these ideas, Murray Bookchin describes the State as something like an image of thought, noting that it is an instilled 'hierarchical mentality' and 'authoritarian outlook fostered by the factory system' to order reality (Biehl 1999: 159). This mentality – this image of thought – structures not only our ways of thinking, but also our relations and desires.[3]

Desire as a category of analysis

One of the most perplexing political problems for Deleuze and Guattari is why and how people come to desire their own repression, or why and how desire comes to be turned against itself (*AO* 32, 63, 105; *ATP* 215). Why, for example, do we desire to live in statist societies when they are so obviously replete with repressive institutions and practices? To try and understand this conundrum, Deleuze and Guattari start by asking questions about how desire becomes invested and arrested – or *machined*, as they would say – by different assemblages in society. In their explanation of how desire is produced, systematized, transformed and circulated, Deleuze and Guattari follow Nietzsche's symptomatological method according to which the entire 'world can be treated as a symptom and searched for signs of disease, signs of life, signs of a cure, signs of health' (*DI* 140). A symptomatology is thus aimed at 'diagnosing' and describing a set of indicators in society, tracing it etiologically and fabulating the best 'therapy' for application – so there is a negative or critical-clinical task embedded in symptomatology as well as a creative and positive project. Call to mind how Nietzsche diagnosed the 'disease' of his society, namely nihilism, by isolating three symptoms – bad conscience, *ressentiment* and the ascetic ideal – only to propose a corrective therapy, namely the revaluation or transvaluation of values.

Similarly, in *Anti-Oedipus*, Deleuze and Guattari diagnose the disease of their society as schizophrenia by isolating capitalist desire. However, before they identify capitalist desire and propose a positive project, they critique the then-predominant framework from which to understand desire, namely psychoanalysis. They especially take umbrage at the way in which psychoanalysis reduces every form of desire – an entire libidinal economy – to a specific familial formation, namely the nuclear family. That is, Oedipal reduction becomes the dogma or image of thought that 'closes the familial triangle over the entire unconscious' so that it no longer 'has anything to do with the social field actually invested by the libido' *(AO* 55, 62). Rather than recognizing that desire is invested in or directed and arrested by myriad arrangements, for instance politics, religion, capitalism, family, friends and popular culture, psychoanalysis synthesizes these desires as stemming from a single source. All 'historical and political content' is thus exclusively and restrictively reduced to the delirium of the family so that the entirety of the external world is generalized as an internal, private and familial problem *(AO* 89). 'There we have it – the incurable familialism of psychoanalysis, enclosing the unconscious within Oedipus, cutting off all vital flows, crushing desiring-production, conditioning the patient to respond daddy-mommy, and to always consume daddy-mommy' *(AO* 92). The point Deleuze and Guattari are driving at is that the psychoanalytic dilution of desire as exclusively Oedipal mistakenly locates the repression of desire in the family when the repressive family is itself an effect of a particular form of social production – in this case, capitalist production *(AO* 118–21). The family thus produces '*a desire that is already submissive and searching to communicate its own submission*' *(K* 10). This, then, is the first critique Deleuze and Guattari have of psychoanalysis: that it arrests desire by cutting off 'all connections, all assemblages', thereby rendering it one-dimensional, which is to say Oedipal *(D* 79). The second critique concerns the way in which psychoanalysis captures our collective capacities to understand desire and the mechanisms by which it becomes repressed and repressive. Because Oedipalized desire acts as a dogmatic image of thought, it symbolically overcodes the chains of expressions that are subsequently produced to understand it. As such, it presents itself axiomatically, thereby constraining our collective thoughts and actions according to the limitations of familial desire when in fact Oedipal desire presupposes capitalist desire.

Silvia Federici gives a good example of this in her analysis of *reproductive labour*. She holds that capitalism is nothing less than a 'war on women' and that the witch-hunts of the sixteenth and seventeenth centuries were central to 'the process that Marx defined as primitive accumulation because it destroyed a universe of female subjects and practices that stood in the way of the main requirements of the developing capitalist system: the accumulation of a massive workforce and the imposition of a more constraining discipline of labor' (2018: 47). The witch hunts were also responsible for a division *between* women because it forced them to become accomplices in the witch-hunts, concurrently instilling and normalizing a hierarchical order that taught women 'above all to accept the place assigned to them' in life (2018: 23). This hierarchical order is carried over to family structures through the subjugation of women to men for capitalist ends which stripped women of their sexual freedoms, often resulting in sexual repression. From a psychoanalytic point of view this repression stems from the Oedipus complex, when in fact Oedipal repression is the result of capitalist oppression.

In making desire their category of analysis, Deleuze and Guattari thus set out not only to understand Oedipalized desire, but also *how* desire came to be reduced to the psychoanalytic form. In so doing, they trace some of the different ways in which desire can become machined, showing especially the difference between nonstate and statist societies, and how the latter produced the right kinds of conditions for capitalism to emerge. In understanding the role of the State for the emergence of capitalism, they depart from Marxists who view the State as little more than a 'sort of protective coating that gives extra cement to the weave of abstraction' brought about by capitalism (Holloway 2010: 95).[4] In this, their analysis is much closer to anarchist views of the State, as we will see.

The coding, overcoding and decoding of fluxes of desire

For a society or community to function as a group rather than as a random assortment of individuals, it has to coordinate and organize its flows or dynamisms – including aspects like food distribution, healthcare practices, sewage and other communal rituals – in such a way that the social field becomes 'invested by desire' (*AO* 262). One of the most direct ways for it to do so is to machine its collective desire through codes, an example of which is *social inscription* or *epigraphy*, which in nonstate societies was often characterized by physical markings like tattoos, brandings and scarifications, or the wearing of masks and the performance of rituals which ensure the autoreproduction of a society through a kind of collective memory by means of these practices. Deleuze and Guattari call this *territorial inscription*, noting that it is based on the collective investment of desire and the shared production of codes of conduct, myths, norms and rules by a society. They are thus examples of more positive and collective ways in which desire can become invested because even though desire is machined or coded in specific ways, it is still heterogeneous and directly invested in and by a society or group. As a mechanism for ensuring inter- and transgenerational memory, it provides a group or society with a certain amount of consistency. The earth, moreover, is not yet striated, meaning the commons are not yet enclosed for the purposes of tax collection by a king or State. Even so, Deleuze and Guattari warn that all inscription processes are what can be thought of as *pharmaka* because they concurrently function as mechanisms for recording or inscription *and* as apparatuses of repression. That is, while territorial inscription retains a high degree of polyvocity or heterogeneity, it produces debt as an apparatus of repression, though this is a debt to society rather than debt as we think of it in capitalist societies (*AO* 184–5). David Graeber illustrates this difference admirably in his book, *Debt*, as we see in Chapter 2.

During the despotic period, or what might be thought of as the time of kings and early States, this changes because the codes generated by groups and societies become *overcoded* through *despotic inscription*. These *reinscription* procedures divest communal desires through 'a second inscription' by the State which appropriates 'all the forces and agents of production' for its own ends (*AO* 235). Instead of desire being invested directly in and by a group or society, it is now invested in society via the State or king – there is thus a layer of representation between people and their desires. Hence, whereas territorial signs and codes were self-validating, and desire was connected in multiple ways, imperial signs and codes begin to abstract and conjugate the production of desire – they are now signs of signs and desires of desires (*AO* 203). This is the first of at least three consequences of overcoding. The second consequence is that the existing polyvocal codes begin to conform to those of the State – and to the image of thought of the State – all the while becoming more homogenized and standardized because overcoding occurs by way of signs that have relatively determined significations (*AO* 194, 196). This does not mean that all existing signs disappear; they are often vestigially retained but are rendered ineffectual or redundant. Think, for example, of how colonial powers used Christianity to overcode local religions. Finally, the 'immanent unity of the earth' gives way 'to a transcendent unity of an altogether different nature – the unity of the State' (*AO* 146). 'Land enters into the sphere of private property and into that of commodities', and class divisions appear (*AO* 218). Debt is transformed into 'a debt of existence, a debt of the existence of the subjects themselves' – a debt payable as tax to the king or State (*AO* 197). In Chapter 3, we will see just how deeply tied the emergence of tax is to the invention of the money form and how it forms one of the three pincers of the State's mechanism of capture alongside rent and profit.

As kings became replaced by States and statecraft became more developed, despotic inscription became intensified as *imperial inscription*, though these organizational shifts described by Deleuze and Guattari should be viewed as formal distinctions not discrete periods with any sort of teleological progression. In reality, these practices and forms of society intersect and overlap, with vestiges of each of the arrangements of socio-political organization and inscription always remaining embedded within and immanent to the new assemblages. Nevertheless, the colonial repositioning of desire does bring about a fluctuation that subordinates desire to 'vengeance' and 'counter-vengeance' – Nietzsche's *ressentiment* – through novel alliances and filiations (*AO* 215). In particular, the law becomes a distinct regime with two features. On the one hand, it is a 'paranoiac-schizoid' metonymic apparatus that functions as the administrative or bureaucratic arm of the State apparatus. On the other, it is a 'maniacal depressive' metaphorical apparatus which conceals its functions by becoming a pure form, *The Law*, with 'no content other than itself' – which is to say its function is not so much to tell 'us what we must do' as it is to inform us of the manner in which our actions need to be modulated to conform to certain subjective rules (*KCP* x). Imperial inscription thus assumes a juridical form (*AO* 202) while debt, for its part, becomes infinite debt through the marriage of the State and religion which turns desire 'against itself' via a machinery of repression. But, as Deleuze and Guattari argue, such desire is *still desire* (*AO* 221).

It is small wonder that the relative freedom of capitalist societies was so enticing. Instead of coding and overcoding, capitalism is marked by decoding and deterritorializing processes that distribute power and modulate desire in original ways (*TR* 28). One of the most significant transitions we see is that the capitalist machine does not function exterior or transcendent to the social system – as is the case between a State and society – but is 'itself determined by the social system into which it is incorporated in the exercise of its functions' (*AO* 221). Basically, the desire of the social machine has melded with the desire of the capitalist machine so that the two desires become 'co-extensive in an immanent process of production' (*AOP* 13). Inscription is transformed once more – this time into a monetary form – but *monetary inscription* is not in itself enough for capitalism to emerge. Capitalism only appears when merchant or financial capital transforms its 'relationship of alliance with noncapitalist production' into a filiative alliance marked by a surplus value. To put it differently, money enters into a relationship with itself according to which money is produced for the sake of money rather than for the acquisition of commodities. That is, 'money begets money' (*AO* 225). This is precisely what makes it filiative because money becomes reproductive in the same way that families are reproductive – for the sake of themselves. In this filiative relation, desire is no longer coded in the ways it was in nonstate societies, nor is it overcoded simply to conform to State ideals, though these types of relation remain vestigial. What we see in capitalist societies is a liberation of the flows of desire, but under specific social conditions that machine desire according to the aims of capitalism. The point Deleuze and Guattari are making is that while capitalism liberated the flows – and 'who doesn't desire flows, and relationships between flows, and breaks in flows?' (*AO* 229) – it simultaneously generated and released new apparatuses of repression which Freud mistakenly identified as a repression of the nuclear family when in fact the 'invention' of the nuclear family was the apparatus of repression produced by capitalism.

These instantiations of the machining of desire are necessarily reductive. The issue at hand is that desire is a *pharmakon* – its investments therefore need to be undertaken with care because the ways in which societies produce, record and reproduce desire greatly affect the kinds of lives that emerge from them. In isolating desire as the category of analysis for their symptomatology, Deleuze and Guattari have as their initial objective a critical-clinical project through which they demonstrate how revolutionary desire becomes subverted or 'sick' in two ways: first through a reformist subversion, or a refusal 'to see it where it exists' and, second, through a dogmatic subversion, by seeing 'it where it manifestly will not occur' (*SS* 8). Moreover, they link the problem of desire – or to be more precise, the question of why and how desire comes to desire its own repression – to what they call *microfascism*, our personal little Oedipuses and dogmatic images of thought, 'microformations' that shape 'postures, attitudes, perceptions, expectations, semiotic systems, etc.' (*ATP* 215). This kind of symptomatology of the microformations of power, marked by their 'molecular and supple segmentarity, flows capable of suffusing every kind of cell' (*ATP* 214), is an insistence 'on the "dark side" of the human psyche – its dependence on power, its identification with authoritarian figures, even its sadistic and aggressive impulses' (Newman 2010a: 61). This is one of the reasons that anarchists have developed a strong critique of the State – because the State apparatus changes society at the level of desire. As Emma Goldman says, States are by their 'very nature conservative, static, intolerant of change and opposed to it', regardless of the form of government they take – 'be it absolute or constitutional, monarchy or republic, Fascist, Nazi or Bolshevik' (Goldman 1996: 115). Its logics, in other words, follow its nature. Anarchists argue, accordingly, that the State is unnecessary and that it necessarily inhibits expressions of freedom through its exploitative and alienating machinery. This is also why anarchists reject 'all forms of government, authority and power', excepting collective self-government, because they understand the corrupting nature of State authority, irrespective of its form of government (Kinna 2005: 81). Rather than being *the* instrument of political life, anarchists hold, likewise, that the State 'is actually the order of depoliticization: it is the structure of power that polices politics by regulating, controlling and repressing the insurgent dimension that is proper to the political; it is a forgetting of the conflict and antagonism at the base of its own foundations' (Newman 2010a: 9). This echoes the distinction made by philosopher Jacques Rancière in *Hatred of Democracy* where he contrasts what he refers to as 'the political' with 'politics', where the *political* refers to the reified political, gendered, racial, economic, classed and other hegemonic structural arrangements and relations of the State apparatus, and *politics* to that which holds the potential for actual or extensive social transformation (Rancière 2006: 33–50). That is to say, the political relations and arrangements of the State, which are 'antagonistic toward individual and collective autonomy', have as their 'foremost aim' the relegation of 'the many to the one, the different to the same, the specific to the general, the particular to the universal, and the concrete to the abstract' (Jun 2019: 37). The State, as part of the political, thus constitutes a whole machinery that orders reality, thought and desire. This machinery is what Deleuze and Guattari describe as the *apparatus of capture*, a concept which, as we see in the next chapter, is developed by them to elaborate the logics and techniques of overcoding, after which we examine the decoding logics of capitalism more closely in Chapter 3.

Tour d'horizon

In this chapter, I argued that Statist realism – or the dogmatic image of thought propagated by the State – posits the State as the horizon of human possibility and so becomes the horizon of the *thinkable*. It is for this very reason that many people find it impossible to imagine life outside of the State, frequently equating such organizations of life derogatively with more 'primitive' social arrangements. We will see in Chapter 2 that this forms a foundational axiom of the State and that part of the power of its dogmatic image of thought stems from the idea that the State evolved from earlier, more 'primitive', forms of social and political organization within which is embedded the false idea that the State is the superior form of socio-political structuring. This idea is seductive for the very reason that it has changed something at the level of desire. Because we think the State is the best possible solution for socio-political arrangements, we desirously produce statist societies, which is why Deleuze and Guattari argue that '*desire is part of the infrastructure*' (*AO* 104). This is the power of Statist realism – that it becomes structural – which is to say it is produced and circulated at the molecular level. Governments, as State forms, thus present molar units of analysis on one end of the scale, whereas Statist realism presents a molecular unit of analysis. As Deleuze and Guattari remind us, it is 'easy to be antifascist on the molar level, and not even see the fascist inside you, the fascist you yourself sustain and nourish and cherish with molecules both personal and collective' (*ATP* 215). And it is precisely this 'fascism in us all, in our heads and in our everyday behavior' that 'causes us to love power, to desire the very thing that dominates and exploits us', as Foucault writes in his preface to *Anti-Oedipus* (*AO* xiii). And yet an analysis or, better, a symptomatology of power is no small task because power is elusive – it does not come neatly packaged, nor is it homogeneous, nor is it easily locatable. Power is, rather, diffuse, 'defined only by the particular points through which it passes' (*F* 25). Understanding how the microfascism of the State works – particularly how it captures and transforms revolutionary desire in all of us – thus necessitates a deeper look at the givens or axiomatics of the State, the logics of the State apparatus and its actualized techniques. This, in turn, requires a denaturalization of the existence of the State. The fact is that *Homo sapiens* only very recently began to live in crowded, sedentary communities with mass-produced agricultural commodities and large concentrations of domesticated livestock governed by States – and yet this seems, and has been touted as, the 'natural' way of things. Peter Gelderloos argues for this reason that the 'question of how and why States were formed is the keystone of Western civilization's creation mythology' (2016: 1). This mythological aspect of the State ensures its normalization in society, the mechanism by which it presents itself to thought as the horizon of human potential; a fully legitimized and unquestionable 'reality' – an invisible dogmatic image that presupposes the State not only as the way things are but the *best way for them to be*. This doxa hinges on a number of axiomatics or givens that 'seal off the lines of flight' and make lines of leakage more difficult. The 'men of State' are 'great axiomaticians' for this reason: they affirm the State as the universal foundation of 'civilized' sociopolitical organization (*ATP* 461). Deleuze and Guattari, like anarchists, have problematized such axioms of the State and, perhaps somewhat surprisingly to many readers, have drawn on overlapping anthropological evidence for their arguments, as we see in the next chapter.

2

Axiomatics of the State

*To be governed is to be at every operation, at every transaction,
noted, registered, counted, taxed, stamped, measured, numbered,
assessed, licensed, authorized, admonished, prevented, reformed,
corrected, punished.*

(Proudhon 1969: 294)

It was in 1521, as the story goes, that the Spanish conquistadors
and their indigenous allies, under the leadership of Hernán Cortés,
defeated the Aztec Empire, made up of an alliance between three city
states – Mexico-Tenochtitlan, Tetzcoco and Tlacopan – though the
allianced lands were largely ruled from Tenochtitlan by the time the
soldiers arrived in 1519. With Spanish appetite for power growing
steadily, the famed Spanish aristocrat, Francisco de Toledo, mounted
another major attack in 1572, this time in Vilcabamba, a region in
Peru that was home to the Sapa Inca people, led by Túpac Amaru,
the last of the Sapa Inca monarchs and second son of Manco Inca
Yupanqui. Although Amaru and his family managed to evade capture
for many months, they were eventually found by a party of soldiers, led
by Martín García Óñez de Loyola, who arrested them and took them
to Cuzco where Amaru was found guilty of the murder of priests.
On 24 September, in a public display characteristic of many colonial
conquests, Amaru was beheaded, his death a symbol of conquest to
those in power and, to those not, an emblem of rebellion. So began
the history of coexistence between indigenous rural peoples and the
mestizo-urban societies of Latin America.

Roughly two centuries later, in 1770, the indigenous communities living in Upper Peru, now Bolivia, experienced intensified economic, social and political hardships as local provincial officials began to be replaced by *mestizos* or outsiders, usually from Spanish descent or with a combined European and indigenous ancestry. This was, in part, aimed at ensuring the smooth implementation of a number of reforms which were supposed to stimulate agricultural, industrial and technological development, and increase trade. These efforts at modernization went hand in hand with the extensive violation of traditional practices, customs and knowledges, as has been the case in many colonized parts of the world. In protest, a local Aymara peasant, Tomás Katari, headed a popular revolt, though he too was apprehended in the end and handed over to the chief magistrate, Juan Antonio Acuña. On their way to La Plata, present-day Sucre, where Katari would be tried, the militia was confronted by a crowd of indigenous people. Acuña, feeling threatened, pushed Katari off a cliff on the heights of the Chataquilla slope. In revenge, Acuña was captured and stoned, his body desecrated and left unburied. Katari's body, on the other hand, was recovered and brought back home where he was given a proper burial. Consequently, a number of local unrest and revolts flared up, igniting a wave of broader regional insurgencies against colonial rule. Amongst these was the 109-day siege of La Paz, led by another Aymara 'commoner', Julián Apaza, who renamed himself Túpac Katari in honour of Túpac Amaru and Tomás Katari. 'The siege was held from various points, and Katari's army', made up of roughly 40,000 indigenous women and men, 'descended to make regular assaults and incursions against the Spanish in La Paz' (Dangl 2019: 4). Although the insurrection shook the Spanish regime, Túpac Katari was detained on 14 November 1781. On 15 November, his limbs 'were tied to the tails of four horses and he was quartered alive' to inspire fear in his followers and any other potential dissenters (Dangl 2019: 4–5). It did not achieve the effect the Spanish may have hoped for.

Although it is very likely apocryphal, it is widely held that, moments before his execution, Túpac Katari uttered the words: 'I will return and there will be millions of us' (Casen 2012: 23). In some sense – if not to the extent of millions – history has shown these words to be prophetic, though it would take nearly another two centuries for the *katarista-indianista* movement to emerge in the La Paz region. Established in the 1960s in opposition to the State's indigenous policies, largely informed by guidelines from the colonial era, Katarismo aimed at creating a State-independent *campesino* workers union that 'directly empowered the rural, indigenous sector rather than the Nationalist Revolutionary Movement (MNR)' (Dangl 2019: 22). The movement, which consisted of a 'rural-urban network of intellectuals, peasant leaders, and grassroots' organizations challenged the 'authoritarian, monopolistic and monocultural' practices of the Bolivian State by calling for 'a new form of democracy, based on the recognition of cultural diversity', as well as 'the right to autonomous self-government by the Indian communities and federations within the structure of the state' (Cusicanqui 2009: 2, 3). But the *kataristas* gained scant access to the largely *mestizo* parliament and the movement gradually became weakened by neoliberal policies. The government, however, paid close attention to *katarista* grievances, co-opting their symbols, ideologies and identity issues for *mestizo* populist party ends. Small wonder hope resurged in 2006 when Evo Morales became Bolivia's first president from indigenous descent. The Morales government even portrayed itself 'as a political force' realizing the 'thwarted dreams of the eighteenth-century indigenous rebel Túpac Katari' (Dangl 2019: 3). Morales also named Bolivia's first satellite and several State-owned planes after Túpac Katari, announcing: 'There you have it in front of you, our legendary 727-200 Boeing, that we are going to name Túpac Katari; he has returned and converted into millions' (quoted in Dangl 2019: 3). To be sure, the Morales government did reduce poverty and empower some marginalized sectors, but even as it advocated for indigenous rights on the one hand, it silenced many grassroots dissidents on the other – especially those who spoke out against the expanding extractive gas and mining industries (Dangl 2019: 2).

These are not novel stories. Innumerable indigenous peoples are familiar with the practices of subjugation, dispossession, genocide, settler colonialism and co-optation, though the specifics and inclusionary-exclusionary mechanisms may differ from place to place and from time to time. Countless peoples are familiar with the erasure of their oral traditions, their unwritten memories of the future, as literacy became 'wielded and monopolized by colonial elites as a tool to rule over the indigenous masses' (Dangl 2019: 13). Too many know the violation of Christianization and alienation, as well as the ensuing lure of formal citizenship – that homogenizing model that exalts universal suffrage and representative democracy as the pinnacle of political achievement, despite overwhelming evidence to the contrary. These stories of progress, modernization and assimilation are the bedrock of the State's apparatus of capture, and the result has been tragic: 'a dependent mentality' that has eroded our individual and collective capacities for self-government (Cusicanqui 1990: 111). This, says Eric Laurson, is the State's greatest achievement: 'to convince us that the State itself is indispensable'; to make us believe 'that any major societal problem, from racism to nuclear proliferation to climate change to affordable housing, can and must be resolved' by the State, and worse, to persuade us that any systemic failure is a 'failure of leadership' rather than a failure of the State itself (2021: ch. 1, para. 8).

In Chapter 1, I diagnosed *statist realism* as that which prevents us from thinking outside or beyond the State apparatus. In this chapter, I look at some of the logics of statist realism, drawing on anarchist analyses, as well as the philosophy of Deleuze and Guattari. As part of my symptomatology, I detail how the State instils a 'unity of composition' via its axiomatic presuppositions which provide it with a certain amount of uniformity despite its historically variable forms, as well as how its 'power of appropriation' works – which does not refer only to its capacities to capture identities, land, natural resources, thoughts and ways of life – but also to the way in which it appropriates the war machine, which is to say the way in which it co-opts anticipation-prevention mechanisms (*ATP* 459, 437). Uncovering these logics, of which statist axioms form a part, is vital because it denaturalizes the idea that the State is necessary and inevitable, as well as the notion that the State form is the best or most progressive structure for socio-political organization which, in turn, unshackles thought from the constraints of statist realism.

The *Urstaat*: The non-chronological origins of the State

AXIOM 1: *The State evolved from earlier, more 'primitive', forms of social and political organization.*

PRESUPPOSITION 1: *The State is the superior form of socio-political organization.*

COROLLARY: *The State – especially when it assumes a democratic or social democratic form – ensures the highest possible expression of individual and collective freedom.*

Political modernization, social civilization and progressivism are some of the foundational presuppositions of the first axiom of the State, all of which assume a teleological or social Darwinian account of socio-political progress from 'hunting and gathering to nomadism to agriculture (and from band to village to town to city)' (Scott 2017: 9). One of the consequences of these embedded assumptions is that even when people recognize 'the basic precepts of multilinear evolution, the historical commonplace of State failure, and the possibility of a stateless complex social organization', temporal idioms are still used that implicitly suggest the supremacy of the State form (Gelderloos 2016: 76). Nonstate societies are, for example, often described as 'early' civilizations or 'primitive' cultures which normalize the idea that the State is the most 'mature' socio-political structure. Embedded in these ideas is a deeply Eurocentric value judgement according to which stateless societies are incomplete, uncivilized and lacking, and 'history is a one-way progression' from 'savagery to civilization', at the end of which is the modern sovereign nation state (Clastres 1989: 189, 190). Yet an investigation into the practices of many nonstate and indigenous societies reveals quite the opposite: that they had multifaceted mechanisms for warding off centralized power formations, including electoral systems that struck a fine balance 'between elements of communal consensus and a compulsory rotating system' that prevented an accumulation of power and wealth (Cusicanqui 1990: 101). Societies, in other words, functioned just fine without the State. It is of course true that some indigenous societies did have State-like forms – the Aztec and Inca were, after all, both expansionist empires. The Inca, moreover, had a centralized economy, although it had complex redistributive requirements, and the society itself was relatively heterogeneous, characterized by numerous local customs and religions. In other words, it was still largely marked by practices of coding. The Spanish State, on the other hand, ruled brutally and hegemonically by overcoding the practices, customs, languages, economies and religions of the indigenous communities they intended to govern, frequently in the name of progress and modernization, as the stories of Túpac Amaru, Tomás Katari and Túpac Katari illustrate. This logic is often extended to the economies of nonstate societies. Accordingly, what imperialists thought of as 'backward' fiscal arrangements that lacked organizational efficiency was in fact a purposeful *refusal* of an economy – nonstate societies produced to satisfy their needs, not to yield a surplus (Clastres 2010: 199). Besides, they did not need to produce excess because there were no external mechanisms, such as the State and capitalism, forcing them to work for a living. It is for this reason that Marshall Sahlins refers to nonstate societies as the 'original affluent societies': because whereas modern statist and capitalist societies, 'however richly endowed, dedicate themselves to the proposition of scarcity', nonstate societies provided enough subsistence for themselves to be satisfied *and* to have leisure time (Sahlins 2017: 4; see also Widerquist and McCall 2017). Poverty, therefore, does not so much connote a 'small amount of goods' or a 'relation between means and ends' as it does a 'social status', a 'relation between people' that was the invention and consequence of the State and capitalism (Sahlins 2017: 36).

A related embedded assumption is that sedentary, State-organized life is necessarily 'superior to and more attractive' than 'mobile forms of existence' but, as James Scott argues, the more archaeological and anthropological research is done, the more hunters and gatherers have 'never looked so good – in terms of their diet, their health, and their leisure' (2017: 8). Agriculturalists, on the contrary, have never looked so bad – 'in terms of *their* diet, *their* health, and *their* leisure' (2017: 10). True, states 'have come to dominate the archaeological and historical record' – which makes it easy to assume 'the permanence of the state and its administered space' as 'an inescapable constant of our condition' – but there are reasons for this, one being that 'a great deal of archaeology and history throughout the world is state-sponsored and often amounts to a narcissistic exercise in self-portraiture' (Scott 2017: 13). This kind of institutional bias is compounded by the fact that more mobile societies were less prone to leave historical ruins and are, as a result, less likely to appear in archaeological records. And anyway, sedentarism and agriculture brought about their own problems – including an unanticipated epidemiological burden, 'not just of people but of livestock, crops, and the large suite of parasites that followed them to the domus or developed there' (Scott 2017: 1821). These include well-known diseases such as the Black Death of the fourteenth century, mumps, measles, diphtheria and Covid-19. Yet despite these obvious disadvantages of sedentary, statist societies, the typological three-stage theory from savagery to barbarism to civilization is one that has become cemented in both lay knowledge and political philosophy. To a great extent this is due to Lewis Henry Morgan's book, *Ancient Society; Or: Researches in the Lines of Human Progress from Savagery through Barbarism to Civilization* (1877), in which progress is presented as inevitable and predetermined stages in human evolution. The work had an enormous influence on many thinkers, including Marx, with the unfortunate effect that this progress narrative spread wide and far, notwithstanding a lack of evidence for linear development (Widerquist and McCall 2017: 114–15). It is far more likely, as David Wengrow and David Graeber have argued, that hunting and gathering societies consciously oscillated 'between contrasting modes of political organisation', depending on their needs and desires at the time (2015: 1). This resonates strongly with Scott's research as well as the anthropological work of anarchist Pierre Clastres who Deleuze and Guattari refer to extensively in their theorization of the State apparatus.

In their work on the State apparatus, Deleuze and Guattari aim to argue, first, that the State did not evolve from earlier socio-political formations and, second, that the State is not a historical necessity. To do so, they develop three interrelated concepts – the *nomadic war machine*, the *Urstaat* and *capture*, the latter two of which are considered in this chapter while the nomadic war machine is discussed in Chapter 6. The theory of the *Urstaat* is first introduced in *Anti-Oedipus* and further developed in *A Thousand Plateaus* to explain how the State 'comes into the world fully formed and rises up in a single stroke' – in other words, how State formation is the result of a qualitative leap and not of an evolutionary process (*ATP* 427; see also *AO* 217). Instead of a teleological view, Deleuze and Guattari argue that statism and nonstatism are immanent to each other – they each form the limit-point for the other after which a threshold is crossed. The *Urstaat* is thus an abstraction, the latent possibility of the State at the limit of statelessness, 'the eternal model of everything the State wants to be and desires' (*AO* 217) – one might even say it is the very *desire* for a transcendent form. Because the *Urstaat* is a latent possibility, always haunting nonstate forms, it cannot be evolutionary in nature. The emergence and genesis of the State only become evolutionary when viewed retrospectively according to statist logic – and that is to confuse the latency of the *Urstaat* with its extensive or actualized forms. The *Urstaat* theory thus challenges evolutionism because, according to it, nonstate societies are not 'primitive' in the sense that 'they failed to reach a certain stage, but are counter-State societies' with 'organizing mechanisms that ward off the State-form' (*ATP* 429) as is accounted for by many anthropological and anarchist studies, including those by Harold Barclay, Peter Gelderloos, David Graeber and James Scott, who outline many of the same issues as Deleuze and Guattari, even though they do not do so in the same specialized, philosophical language. Having said that, the *Urstaat* theory does provoke a question: How is it possible to ward off the State-form if it is only a latency? How would nonstate peoples 'know' what to ward off?

In addressing this question Deleuze and Guattari argue, following Clastres, that nonstate societies were societies *against* the State – rather than societies who merely *lacked* a State – because they actively divested centralized power through their organizational mechanisms, such as an absence of social stratification – which is to say that division is not in any way 'inherent in the social being' (Clastres 2010: 170) – and the disjoining of power and prestige. *Society against the State* thus expresses both a critical project and a positive one. On the one hand, it articulates a 'modality of collective life based on the symbolic neutralization of political authority and the structural inhibition of ever-present tendencies to convert power, wealth and prestige into coercion, inequality and exploitation', and on the other, it speaks to a 'politics of intergroup alliance guided by the strategic imperative of local, community-centered autonomy' (Viveiros de Castro 2010: 12). Drawing on his anthropological observations of a number of Amazonian cultures, Clastres argues that a 'tribal chief does not prefigure the chief of State' because there are entirely different logics at play (1989: 206). While chiefs enjoy prestige, they have no political power: the chief is there to serve society rather than rule it, so the society itself is the true locus of power 'that exercises its authority over the chief' (Clastres 1989: 207; see also Barclay 2002: 54).

A contemporary example of this can be found in the Zapatistas, an indigenous movement in Mexico's southeastern state of Chiapas who practice *mandar obedeciendo*, or 'leading by obeying', according to which leaders, similarly to the chiefs described by Clastres, are deprived of their power in that they govern by submitting their authority to the collective decisions of their communities. The desire of the communities is, accordingly, coded directly by them, not via representational mechanisms. What is being warded off is not so much the State itself as the anticipation of how a particular form of organization and representation founded on centralized power structures will disempower a society – so 'warding off' is the act of anticipating a different 'threshold of consistency' (*ATP* 432, 434). The point that Clastres, and Deleuze and Guattari in their later theorizations, are driving at is that the privileged economic rationality of retrospective statist thinking grounded in a Eurocentric bias denies the political intentionality of nonstate societies.[1] Moreover, Clastres's image of a society against the State gives to us a new image of thought – another image 'of economy, of culture, of sociality, of politics' (Viveiros de Castro 2010: 26). This new image of thought undermines progressivism by demonstrating that the State is neither the most advanced form of socio-political organization, nor necessarily the best structure for ensuring the highest possible expression of freedom through representative democracy. Consider, for a moment, the democratic ideal and the machinery of representative rule and majority vote. The only way it differs from 'absolute monarchy and the totalitarian state' is that instead of people placing 'their trust in a single leader, democracy elevates the majority decision of the populace to a divine status, even though it rarely ever actually implements it' (Barclay 2002: 46). Moreover, marginal voices are necessarily precluded through majority vote. Nonstate societies, as Sahlins, Clastres, Scott and Graeber have argued, thus enjoyed far greater freedom than we do because it is in the nature of the State apparatus to constrain freedom and self-determination. We have simply become *conditioned* to think that human communities cannot govern themselves and work together to ensure the maximum amount of freedom for all. This impression is cultivated not only via notions of progress, civilization and modernization, but also via the second interrelated axiom which posits that the emergence of the State was a necessary, rather than contingent, development.

The apparatus of capture: The contingent nature and primary violence of the State

AXIOM 2:   *The history of the State is a universal history of necessity.*
PRESUPPOSITION 1:   *The State saves humans from their own violent natures.*
COROLLORY: *The violence of the State is secondary and legitimate.*

The second axiom, according to which the State evolved from necessity rather than contingent conditions, is one that is deeply embedded in political philosophy, grounded in the views of Enlightenment thinkers like Thomas Hobbes, John Locke and David Hume. Hobbes's views, expressed in *Leviathan*, first published in English in 1651, paints a picture of a dog-eat-dog world wherein the State is a survival measure aimed at protecting people from their most brutish natures. The idea that people were driven 'by self-interest' and that society only emerged when people came to realize 'that it is to their long-term advantage to give up a portion of their liberties and accept the absolute power of the King' might even 'be considered the opening salvo of the new moral perspective' of the Enlightenment – 'and it was a devastating one' (Graeber 2011: 331). For it was in large part Hobbes's state of nature as a state of war that gave credence to the presupposition that state violence – both its originary violence and its subsequent monopoly on the 'legitimate' use of force – is secondary and justifiable.[2] Hobbes's understanding of 'primitive' societies as warring also led him to conclude that they were lacking in moral character.[3] He argued, accordingly, that morality only came into existence through the 'social contract', a *de jure* account of authority according to which there is an implied consent in society. That is, 'anyone who chooses to live in a particular political community incurs an implicit obligation to comply with the government of that community' so that 'the government has *de jure* authority over anyone who refrains from explicitly rejecting that authority' (Jun 2019: 40). Anarchists have long been critical of the idea of a social contract. Kropotkin, for example, thought that the social contract was little more than 'a weapon with which to fight the divine rights of kings', meaning the social contract itself was an apparatus of capture because it justified the existence of the State as deific and therefore as preordained (1896). Proudhon, for his part, argued that Rousseau 'understood nothing of the social contract' (1851). If anything, he held, the social contract was an explicit agreement of mutual aid and solidarity between people themselves from which a society emerged, rather than an implicit agreement between the government and the people. Bakunin went as far as to call the social contract an 'absurd fiction' and hoax' that binds humans 'into perpetual slavery' when in fact it was the State that corrupted communal solidarity by uniting some, via the enticement of citizenship, 'in order to destroy, conquer, and enslave all the rest' (1953). Here Bakunin is also exposing a 'central paradox in the theory of the social contract: if, in a state of nature, individuals subsist in a state of primitive savagery, then how can they suddenly have the foresight to come together and create a social contract?' (Newman 2006).

To situate this kind of justification of the State, Scott links it to what he calls 'high-modernist ideology' in his seminal text, *Seeing Like a State*. Essentially, this set of optimistic, if oftentimes uncritical, beliefs about 'progress' brought about a fundamental shift in how the State was perceived. 'Before then, the state's activities had been largely confined to those that contributed to the wealth and power of the sovereign', but the advancement in science and technology in especially the industrialized parts of the world – specifically Western Europe and the United States between 1830 and the First World War – brought with it the 'idea that one of the central purposes of the state was the improvement of all the members of society' (Scott 1998: 91). The shift was commutual: even as the populace changed their views about the State, the State shifted its views about social engineering. No longer was the welfare of society merely a means to attain national unity and power, it was now increasingly seen as an end in itself; a 'state that improved its population's skills, vigor, civic morals, and work habits would increase its tax base and field better armies' (Scott 1998: 91). High modernism on the part of the State is thus a far-reaching vision of how technical and scientific progress might be inserted through statecraft into 'every field of human activity', whereas on the part of society it is the Enlightenment ideology that an improved society is the very 'perfectibility of social order' (Scott 1998: 90, 93). This provokes the assumption that societies *naturally* tended towards State societies; that is to say, because stateless societies were seen as savage, primitive and barbaric, State formation came to be viewed as a *necessary* intervention which led to nonviolent, modern societies – in a nutshell, *progressive* civilizations. The corollary of this kind of thinking is that all State violence is secondary to societal violence and therefore legitimate. It is not surprising, then, that a large portion of the world population believes that the State 'is a benign institution which aims to provide a variety of essential services', including the provision of security, health, education, sustenance and other desirable commodities and public ministrations (Barclay 2002: 9).

Much anthropological – and anarchist anthropological – work has shown this to be incorrect or seriously misleading: the State neither saved people from 'survival in a dog-eat-dog world', nor was it *at any point* 'the result of a consensual process designed to protect people's liberties and well-being' (Gelderloos 2016: 3). The State was neither necessary nor inevitable; it was, rather, as studies by Clastres and Scott show, a contested social form that emerged from contingent conditions. Moreover, the State established itself on a principle of violence, 'creating a concentrated monopoly on power' by 'claiming sole legitimacy and authority' and 'supporting unequal class hierarchies, inequalities of wealth and economically exploitative practices' (Newman 2010a: 24). It is for these reasons that Deleuze and Guattari conceptualize the State apparatus as an *apparatus of capture*: first, because it quite literally 'captures' the earth – plants and animals included – and its people through rent, profit and taxation (*ATP* 444); second, because it captures thought to naturalize the idea that the State is a benevolent institution without which society would be immoral and bestial; and finally, because it also captures its opposition, oftentimes through co-optation, as we saw with the Morales government and the *kataristas*. In order to capture something – like land, for example – the State apparatus erects itself in that milieu and posits itself as the foundation thereof. Basically, it creates what it wants to capture. For example, if it wants to capture land, it striates land and creates property, then claims that the land and property belonged to the State to begin with. The colonial enterprise is replete with examples of this kind of seizure. Deleuze and Guattari, like anarchists, see this as the originary or primary violence of the State – its 'preaccomplished and self-presupposing' or 'magic' nature (*ATP* 427). Once it has magically – which really means violently – captured what it wants, the State apparatus performs a second violence through overcoding via its *regime of signs* (*ATP* 428). Recall that overcoding is a reinscription process aimed at legibility and simplification to ensure social subjection. These overcoding logics operate *semiologically* rather than linguistically because the sign flows are asignifying; that is, they bypass signification by acting directly on material flows as power signs. In this way they subjugate and conform all expressions to the image of the State, either by appropriating other signs or making heterogeneous points – such as culture, politics, language and economy – resonate with its own signs (*ATP* 445). This is how the State apparatus changes the nature of an assemblage: it crosses a threshold of consistency by deterritorializing existing codes, overcoding them and so creating its own *intraconsistency* through resonance (*ATP* 433). Signs are thus doubly articulated because a 'sign always refers to another sign, indefinitely' and 'the supposedly infinite ensemble of signs itself refers to a greater signifier', namely the State (*TR* 14).

A practical example of how the State overcodes can be found in legibility practices which imply, first of all, 'a viewer whose place is central and whose vision is synoptic' – it is therefore necessarily a simplification process, though one that is deeply entwined with power (Scott 1998: 79). Anarchists have long argued that 'the instruments that governments use to enforce authority' (Kinna 2005: 58), such as the law, political and economic structures, the police and military, ideology, nationalism *and administration*, demonstrate that the State 'is the site where power is at its most concentrated, excessive and brutal', even though power is not reducible to the State (Newman 2010a: 62). The exertion of power, moreover, deeply affects our lives, often in unseen ways, because the 'cities we live in, political institutions, cultural patterns, and group behaviors all are living forces around us that are greater than the sums of the individuals within them, and in fact make up part of how we become who we are' (Nappalos 2019: 70). That is, we inhabit spaces that stratify, segment, order, care for and revive – or *shape* – us, in various ways. Many anarchists have associated power with enslavement, the restriction of freedom, arbitrary authority and the State's transformation of the very nature of a society, though most anarchists see power as being organized and exerted both negatively and positively. So, whereas the State's organization and exertion of power are seen as examples of negative power or power *over* – what Deleuze and Guattari call *pouvoir* – power *to* or *puissance* expresses positively potentiated power, for example the power to create, the power to effect social change and the power to love. According to Deleuze and Guattari, power functions through centres of resonance which ensure communication between disparate spheres, all of which conform to the image of the State. The nuclear family can therefore be seen to function as a mini-State which is reflected back to itself through the Church, and becomes reinforced at school, university, the workplace, *ad infinitum*. All of these centres of resonance form part of what Scott calls the 'social engineering' practices of the State (1998: 183), which Gelderloos articulates more dramatically as 'social war' (2016: 105). One of the techniques that ensure communication between these centres is legibility, a central problem in statecraft which not only ensures resonance but can be seen as the very inception of political surveillance since it renders space manageable and human action predictable through subjectification processes which engender patterned behaviours and thoughts that are externally managed through reward-punishment mechanisms.

The cadastral map was one of the earliest techniques of legibility. 'Created by trained surveyors and mapped to a given scale, the cadastral map is a more or less complete and accurate survey of all landholdings' aimed at creating a reliable enough representation of a given area (Scott 1998: 36). It is thus a recorded abstraction and miniaturization of the relationship between space and people, one that changed the expression of society by adding a 'documentary intelligence to state power' (Scott 1998: 39). This documentary intelligence could not have developed as it had without 'a system of innovation in writing' (*ATP* 382), which is also why other systems, such as oral ones, were devalued in statist societies. This is not to say these practices were uncontested – resistance 'came not only from the general population but also from local power-holders' who 'were frequently able to take advantage of the administrative incoherence produced by differing interests and missions within the ranks of officialdom' (Scott 1998: 24). In the end, though, mapmaking, along with the adoption of other uniform measurements, prevailed. And it is precisely the cadastral map which made the administration of rent, profit and taxation – the three elements of capture discussed by Deleuze and Guattari – possible.

Rent only became viable once the earth was striated and territorialized according to the spatial and enclosing logics of the apparatus of capture. Through techniques like the cadastral map, abstract, 'smooth' and borderless space became metricized space with plots of land enclosed by fences, countries by borders, nations by nationalities, and so on. 'It is a vital concern of every State not only to vanquish nomadism but to control migrations and, more generally, to establish a zone of rights over an entire "exterior", over all of the flows traversing' the bordered region (*ATP* 385). These borders are harnessed by States to reinforce antagonisms, such as racial and economic animosities, via rhetoric centred on citizenship, nationalism and xenophobia, often to mask the State's own inability to deal with its poorer populations. Think, for example, of Donald Trump's promises to build a wall between the United States and Mexico which was intended mainly to 'buy the allegiance of white people, even desperately poor white people, by giving them scapegoats at whom they' could 'channel their frustration' (CrimethInc. 2018). The capturing of the earth thus constitutes the gridding and demarcation of land, a procedure that is 'inseparable from a process of relative deterritorialization' and which places the State in a position to demand rent (*ATP* 441). But striation is not only effectuated on the earth; it also becomes a mode of thought, the *cogitatio universalis* that operates according to universals and grounds 'itself in an all-encompassing totality' (*ATP* 377, 379) – a dogmatic image of thought – so that the existence of the State and its capturing of the earth are normalized and even justified, as we see in Hobbes. With space captured, boundaried, layered and overlayed through maps and other documenting techniques, the idea of 'land' is invented and the technique of ground rent becomes deployed. Striation also renders the legibility of human activity easier because the activities of a specific person or group of persons become coupled with a finite piece of land. But this only occurs when human activity is captured through a specific form of labour, namely *surplus labour* – a form of labour from which the State recuperates interest or profit, though this is itself reliant on stratification and segmentation logics (*ATP* 444).

For the State to impose rent, it is necessary to distinguish between those who collect rent and those who pay rent, those who own the means of production and those who work to produce surplus. The procedures of capture that ensure this kind of social division are segmentation and stratification, the latter of which divides the earth, but also people, into strata with relations between them (*ATP* 269). Stratification, like any operation of the State, also functions via a number of overcoding techniques, one of which is *faciality* – an ascription process according to which people are categorized so that their trajectories become pre-conditioned. The way it works is that the face becomes 'detached' from the body and overcoded so that all ensuing subjectivities are pre- and over-determined. The most obvious example of faciality is race which operates according to a reasoning that determines 'degrees of deviance' between a predetermined centre and its margins. With the invention of race, the White man's face became centred – specifically the Europeanized Jesus-face – which made it easy to spot traits that did not conform to this image, because any centred image 'propagates waves of sameness until those who resist identification have been wiped out' or subjugated (*ATP* 178). This 'deviance' from the centre is also exploited to justify the ascendancy of some over others. Another example, which was also a necessary precondition for the development of modern statecraft, was the creation of 'permanent, inherited patronyms' – an administrative simplification that rendered people legible for purposes such as tax, conscription and property deeds (Scott 1998: 65). This went hand in hand with the 'development of written, official documents such as tithe records, manorial dues rolls, marriage registers, censuses, tax records, and land records' without which the efficient management of rent, profit and taxation would be near impossible (Scott 1998: 67). The imposition of permanent surnames was also employed to control women and people of colour, especially during the colonial years – though this of course continues in our contemporary societies, albeit in somewhat altered forms, for example migration. The actual practices through which life becomes stratified are, undoubtedly, far more complex than what may appear here, and stratification is almost always contested. Moreover, it works in tandem with other measures, like segmentarity, a kind of compartmentalization or classification logic 'inherent to all the strata composing us' (*ATP* 208).

Segmentation occurs in a number of ways. First, we are segmented in a *binary* fashion – this kind of segmentation usually affects subjectivity directly as it follows 'the great major dualist oppositions: social classes, but also men-women, adults-children', humans-nonhumans, owners-workers and so on (*ATP* 208). We are also segmented in a *circular* fashion through subdivisions that bind us to the earth or land in 'ever larger circles, ever wider disks or coronas', for example a neighbourhood, a city, a province, a country and so on (*ATP* 208–9). Finally, we are segmented in a *linear* fashion, 'along a straight line or a number of straight lines, of which each segment represents an episode or "proceeding": as soon as we finish one proceeding we begin another, forever proceduring or procedured, in the family, in school, in the army, on the job' (*ATP* 209). This is what Foucault described as discipline – a form of governmentality essential to the preservation of the State. Discipline, in other words, is a kind of power – a technology of power really – that traverses different spheres but makes them converge and resonate. To do so, it creates a type of closed system marked by discreet but procedural spaces, such as the school, the prison, the factory, hospitals and the barracks where bodies could be concentrated, distributed in space and ordered in time in order to produce a productive, homogenous and disciplined workforce or prison population, with clock-in/clock-out systems being exemplary of the kind of penal apparatus installed in such spaces (*F* 26, Deleuze 1992b: 5–6). As we will see in Chapter 4, Deleuze, close to the end of his life, begins to see this kind of segmentarity as being more vestigial by the end of the 1990s and being superseded by another form of governmentality which becomes more dominant, namely control, which functions according to modulation rather than specialization. At any rate, the point is that all the measurements taken by the State to ensure its own reproduction reduce the complexity of life so that the polyphonic rhythms of life are increasingly metricized as more redundancies are propagated through the entire social field.

The final aspect of capture discussed by Deleuze and Guattari is taxation, which captures the economy through money so that a pecuniary logic of debt becomes adopted. Taxation, in other words, is what monetarizes the economy and is, as such, deeply tied to the invention of the money form as well as the criminalization of debt, as we see in Chapter 3.

Tour d'horizon

This chapter should have made clear why – and contrary to Marxists – anarchists, and Deleuze and Guattari think that the State is more than a layer of abstraction that lends authority to capitalism, and that it 'developed as an independent force in history, separate from the system of economic exploitation that it functioned to uphold' (Kinna 2005: 30). Accordingly, anarchists view the State as a violent institution which begets always more violence. It is not, as is commonly held in political philosophy, a necessary measure that emerged to safeguard people from their most inhumane proclivities. The State was neither necessary nor inevitable, but a contested structure that emerged from contingent conditions, which is to say it did not develop teleologically from more 'primitive' structures. It marks, rather, a qualitative leap in history – one which was forcefully imposed through mechanisms of capture, as is exemplified by the opening tales of Túpac Amaru, Tomás Katari and Túpac Katari. The State, moreover, is upheld by several myths which have become axiomatic, meaning they have become accepted as factual. One of these is the theory of the social contract, according to which individuals implicitly consent to relinquish some of their freedoms to the State in order to enjoy a greater sense of security vis-à-vis the State's maintenance of social order – which a society or community is presumably incapable of organizing on its own. But, as we saw, it was in fact the State that created the dissent it was supposedly guarding people against, which it accomplished through its apparatus of capture – an exploitative mechanism that extracts resources from the earth and people alike. As the State striates land to create private property, a new kind of relationship between people, the natural world and objects is induced, in turn making it possible for the State to impose rent. This division of the earth takes place in tandem with the stratification of the social body which sorts people into hierarchized categories, the lower of which form the workforce whose surplus labour is converted into profit for the State. Through these capturing techniques the State increasingly gains control of all the available resources in a society, so concentrating wealth in the hands of the few at the expense of the many. As lands and peoples become cumulatively regimented, measured, domesticated and disciplined through complex reward-punishment and native-alien mechanisms, certain figures are produced, for example 'citizens' and 'migrants', the latter of which is often used by the State to justify its monopoly on force through rhetoric of 'foreign invasion', which is then used to rationalize the existence of violent State institutions, like the military and police.

All good and well, you might be thinking, but what happens when societies become too large and complex? Do they not 'naturally' start requiring a State-like structure? The first answer to this question is that even if societies are large and complex, they can still function very well with more decentralized forms of organization, as the Zapatistas and the Kurdish Freedom Movement in Rojava demonstrate. The Zapatistas, for example, follow a model of 'good-government juntas' and autonomous municipalities, both of which have 'slightly different rules and methods of rotation' because while the municipalities are coordinated by regional juntas, they remain self-governing (Starr, Martínez-Torres and Rosset 2011: 105). The rotational system, which is designed to demystify governmental processes by giving 'every Zapatista the experience of government', is also defined by free service 'on a junta or in any other position of authority or service' which prevents the accumulation of power, money and prestige, thus also limiting – and even eradicating – corruption (Starr, Martínez-Torres and Rosset 2011: 105). Similarly, the Kurdish Freedom Movement – initiated in 2014 by Kurdish forces in resistance to the Islamic State of Iraq and Syria (ISIS) during the Siege of Syria – rejects the nation-state in favour of citizen assemblies and confederalism, ideas put forward by the anarchist Murray Bookchin which had a profound influence on Abdullah Öcalan, the founding member of the militant Kurdistan Workers' Party (PKK). The Kurdish Freedom Movement, accordingly, bases their organization on principles of 'democratic confederalism' which they see as a 'grassroots task' according to which people manage themselves by organizing themselves through direct democracy at community level (Baher 2018). The second answer in some ways precedes the first and turns the question on its head by revealing that 'the unprecedented concentrations of domesticated plants, animals, and people that characterize states' is anything but natural (Scott 2017: 5). A brief foray into deep history reveals that sedentary societies with crop domestications predate the emergence of the State by about four millennia – so relatively multifaceted societies, at least in terms of demographic conditions and technological requirements for crop domestication, existed for an exceptionally long period without needing a State. The 'very first small, stratified, tax-collecting, walled states' only appear around 3,100 BCE in the Tigris and Euphrates Valley and these and similar States were contested for a long time as is verified by the 'massive evidence of determined resistance by mobile peoples everywhere to permanent settlement, even under relatively favorable circumstances' (Scott 2017: 6, 8). The shift from hunting-gathering to agriculture did, in other words, not take place naturally, easily or swiftly and it came with at least as many costs as gains. What is striking, though, is 'that virtually all classical states were based on grain, including millets. History records no cassava states, no sago, yam, taro, plantain, breadfruit, or sweet potato states', which Scott argues is most likely because 'only grains are best suited to concentrated production, tax assessment, appropriation, cadastral surveys, storage, and rationing' (Scott 2017: 21). State formation, it would seem, only becomes possible when land is striated, people stratified and dietary alternatives restricted and dominated by domesticated grains which are easily taxable. Because food sources become taxable, people become more concentrated on land where food is produced which leads to complexification and expansion, both of which are then used retrospectively by the State to justify its existence. In the next chapter we take a closer look at what Deleuze and Guattari say about tax and why they argue that it forms the third prong of the apparatus of capture along with rent and profit.

3

Capital: A nervous condition

An initial disorientation: there is something wrong in our lives, a recurrent feeling that things are deeply off balance; so off balance, it seems, that the ability to return to balance, or even to say what balance was or will be, is compromised. What is wrong in our lives overruns the easy synonyms we have for wrong, words like oppression, domination, and exploitation.

(Austin Anarchist Study Group 2012)

To re-read a landscape we have always read as capitalist, to read it as a landscape of difference, populated by various capitalist and noncapitalist economic practices and institutions – that is a difficult task. It requires us to contend not only with our colonized imaginations, but with our beliefs about politics, understandings of power, conceptions of economy, and structures of desire.

(C. C. Williams, *A Commodified World? Mapping the Limits of Capitalism*, 2005, Zed Books, used by permission of Bloomsbury Publishing Plc.)

In a letter to Jean-Baptiste Leroy, dated 13 November 1789, Benjamin Franklin wrote a line that has become an oft-cited truism: that nothing in this world is certain, except death and taxes. He should have added tax dodges. Remember the Panama Papers?[1] Surpassing even the intelligence documents made available by Edward Snowden, the Panama Papers was an unprecedented leak of 11.5 million financial and legal documents for more than 214,488 offshore entities from the database of one of the world's largest offshore law firms, Mossack Fonseca. Sending shock waves through the world, it revealed how shell corporations set up by the firm were used to bypass international sanctions and take advantage of cryptic offshore tax regimes. Somewhat unsurprisingly, the leaked files implicated 143 politicians, their associates and family members, including former British Prime Minister David Cameron; former Icelandic Prime Minister Sigmundur Davíð Gunnlaugsson, former Ukraine President Petro Poroshenko, the then-incumbent Prime Minister of Pakistan, Nawaz Sharif, and his brother, Shehbaz Sharif; and the current Russian President, Vladimir Putin (Harding 2016; Fitzgibbon and Hudson 2021). Although the Kremlin dismissed the leaks as 'Putinphobia' and life in Russia continued largely unperturbed, protests erupted in other parts of the world, with demonstrators throwing rocks in Pakistan, and bananas, eggs and yoghurt in Iceland. Londoners, meanwhile, brandished placards and donned Suidae masks – a reminder of Cameron's 'pig gate' scandal based on an allegation that he inserted his male member into the mouth of a dead pig as part of an initiation ceremony whilst a student at Oxford University. That aside, the protests achieved some significant results: Sigmundur Davíð Gunnlaugsson resigned and, in what would become *the* landmark Panamagate case, officially titled *Imran Ahmed Khan Niazi v. Mian Muhammad Nawaz Sharif*, the Supreme Court of Pakistan made a historic decision that disqualified Nawaz Sharif from holding public office for life. Yet despite these victories and continued advocacy for transparency prompted by the Panama Papers leaks, tax policies remain structurally inclined towards the affluent and tax havens the playground of the rich. It is no secret that Donald Trump, who likes to punt himself as the poster boy of the self-made man, received about $413 million in today's currency from his father's real estate empire, much of it through tax circumvention (Barstow, Craig and Buettner 2018).

In their policy analysis report, 'Overcoming the Shadow Economy', Joseph Stiglitz and Mark Pieth respond to the growing global concerns prompted by the Panama Papers over secrecy-havens – 'jurisdictions in which global financial flows' are 'hidden in ways that not even those entrusted with enforcing the laws and regulations of countries around the world' can detect (2016: 3). Because of such opacities, these havens facilitate activities like the laundering of money and tax evasion which contribute to excessively high levels of wealth disparity. In an effort to curb these and other related challenges, Stiglitz and Pieth call for new global standards, including freely accessible and searchable registries listing the beneficial owners of all corporations; whistle-blower protection and a strong Freedom of Information Act (FOIA) which they hold is central for transparency and meaningful citizen participation and engagement; annual public reports; and limiting the number of boards or management positions that nominee directors and officers may hold (Stiglitz and Pieth 2016: 15, 18–20). The document, while shedding light on a number of egregious misuses enabled by secrecy-havens and suggesting some admirable reforms, hardly addresses the structural causes of wealth inequalities, nor does it question the assumed legitimacy of tax collection. This, argues David Graeber, is the 'real weak link in state-credit theories': that they try to explain the reasons for tax implementation by early States – which was to create markets – but fail to ask 'by what right?' they could do so (2011: 55).

This is a question Deleuze and Guattari respond to in their theorization of tax. According to them, the enforcement of tax is, alongside rent and profit, a prerequisite for the State capture of the earth and people, as we began to see in Chapter 2. It is also profoundly entwined with the invention of the money form. Deleuze and Guattari hold in fact that 'money presupposes taxation' (*ATP* 428), which is another way of saying that taxation – not commerce or markets – provoked the need for money. Once the money-form was 'thus derived from taxation', and established as the standard medium of exchange, it made 'possible a monopolistic appropriation of outside exchange by the State' insofar as it captured trade (*ATP* 443). In other words, the invention and standardization of money enabled the State to capture trade via tax *and* invent foreign trade which, in turn, allowed the State to claim tax on trade – both within the boundaries of their territory and outside of it. This is why tax forms the third aspect of the 'trinity formula' of the apparatus of capture alongside rent and profit: because it not only captures trade but also the economy by monetizing it, thus incurring a pecuniary logic of debt which is always, primarily, a debt to the State. Moreover, it creates a situation where money begins to be produced for the sake of more money.

As with the State, tax has become clouded in myth – an image of thought – prompted in large by Adam Smith, intellectual heir to liberal philosophers like John Locke, whose propertarian theory posits that 'a commons is naturally available for appropriation', though the manner in which 'appropriators establish property rights' and the means by which they give themselves 'the moral authority to do so remains controversial even among propertarians' (Widerquist and McCall 2017: 68). The point remains that proprietors, by whatever moral justification, claim it as their 'natural' right to use a seized commons for whatsoever reason they may desire – be that for building a family home that can be bequeathed, or real estate speculation. Adams also argued that money was not the creation of the State, insisting instead that barter and exchange are the 'natural' proclivities of humans. Left to their own devices, he argued, humans will always try to get the most profitable outcome from any exchange. In his words, barter is 'a certain propensity in human nature' involving the 'exchange of one thing for another' (1976: 25). The outcome? Everyone starts stockpiling: territory is stockpiled as enclosed land, activity is stockpiled as tools and exchange is stockpiled as money (*ATP* 444). Except, according to Deleuze and Guattari, stock is not derived directly from territory, activity or exchange as Smith would have it; rather, it is *produced by* the apparatus of capture. As we saw in Chapter 2, the State creates what it wants to capture. Land is striated and stratified to 'invent' property which is then captured by the State who claims the territory as its own and charges *rent*. People are stratified and segmentalized to 'invent' non-citizens and citizens, the latter of whom the State captures by claiming that said persons belonged to the State to begin with. Because they belong to the State, those classified as labourers have to work for the State, producing surplus to be converted into *profit*. This still leaves room for people to trade – so tax is invented to capture trade, both local and foreign, but it does not only capture trade, it captures the entire economy by overcoding all commercial activities.[2] This is the *economic* function of the State: protecting private property and accumulating capital by way of tax enforcement. This is also how the State ensures its own autoreproduction because we 'create and re-create the state by paying taxes' (Holloway 2010: 134). It is for this reason that Proudhon argues that even though tax is 'sustained by the *proletaire*', it 'belongs to that great family of preventive, coercive, repressive, and vindictive institutions' established by the State (2012: 317).

Debt and the logics of enclosure

Where Deleuze and Guattari provide the theoretical underpinnings for tax as an apparatus of capture, Graeber, in his seminal text, *Debt: The First 5,000 Years*, provides anthropological evidence to discredit Smith's 'natural barter tendency' hypothesis. Drawing on a range of theorists, including Caroline Humphrey, the authoritative scholar on barter economy, Graeber argues that no 'example of a barter economy, pure and simple, has ever been described, let alone the emergence of money from it; all available ethnography suggests that there never has been such a thing' (Humphrey quoted in Graeber 2011: 29). This is not to say that people did not barter; they did, but not in an economized manner, and not between fellow villagers or with the 'savages' imagined by Smith – stateless societies tended to be without market economies after all. When barter did take place, it was usually exacted between strangers or enemies with the aim of trading objects of *equivalence*. The implication is that when one object is exchanged for a counter-object, 'each of the two parties is equally free to walk away' because no further association is required. Exchange thus 'allows us to cancel out our debts' (Graeber 2011: 104). Conversely, relationality requires *inequivalence*. For example, I invite a friend over for dinner. She brings a bottle of wine. Next time we see each other we go for coffee and I offer to pay. A few weeks later she invites me over to listen to records. We order food and split the bill. Subsequently we end up going to the movies and she pays. At no point is an equivalent gesture required. As Graeber explains: to 'bring back nothing at all would be to cast oneself as an exploiter or a parasite'; to 'bring back an exact equivalent would be to suggest that one no longer wishes to have anything to do' with the other person because friendship and community relationship are not founded on debt as we have come to understand it (2011: 105). Barter, moreover, did not give rise to the invention of money. 'We did not begin with barter, discover money, and then eventually develop credit systems. It happened precisely the other way around. What we now call virtual money came first. Coins came much later, and their use spread only unevenly, never completely replacing credit systems' (Graeber 2011: 40). But whatever its origins, money has, for at least the last 4000 years, been a relation of debt to the State, though this has been a contested relation and one that only came about when debt became *criminalized* (Graeber 2011: 334). Before that debt was simply an exchange that had not been brought to completion and bound people of potentially equal standing to each other in specific ways. When debt became criminalized, however, it assumed a different, more hierarchical relationship between people, at once shifting something at the level of desire – as Graeber himself says in rather Deleuzoguattarian vocabulary. 'We might say, then, that money introduced a democratization of desire', at least insofar 'as everyone wanted money, everyone, high and low, was pursuing the same promiscuous substance' (Graeber 2011: 190). Soon, however, people not only wanted money; they needed it. Whereas coinage arose independently, though almost simultaneously, in three places – northern China, northeast India and the lands bordering the Aegean Sea – capitalism only emerged when 'an economy of credit was converted into an economy of interest' (Graeber 2011: 332), and this only came about when debt was criminalized via taxation, actualized through the creation of the cadastral map, land register and birth registry (Scott 1998: 38).

If legibility is a central problem of statecraft and the cadastral map one of the earliest techniques of legibility, taxation is the driving logic behind the creation of the map. And it is precisely this combination of primitive 'accumulation qua stratification' that constitutes the apparatus of capture (Protevi 2019: 27). One might say that stratification was the Originary violence of the State, whereas tax obligations were the secondary violence incurred from the first. This dramatically altered how we think about and perform work because labour did not exist as a monetary relation *separated from other life activities* before the emergence of the State. So work, as we understand it today, is first and foremost an operation of imperial bureaucracy that forms part of the 'calculation techniques that were springing up at the border between mathematical science and social technology (there is a whole social calculus at the basis of political economy, demography, the organization of work, etc.)' (*ATP* 389). But the aim of such social engineering was always taxation – the monetization of social relations through a 'constant process of stratification' which invites 'social conflict' that was utilized retrospectively by the State to justify its own existence (Holloway 2010: 168). Taxes, moreover, augur capitalism because the apparatus of capture introduces a new regime of signs, namely *social subjection*, according to which humans are subjected '*to* the machine and no longer enslaved *by* the machine' – so social subjection functions alongside *machinic enslavement*, or what might be thought of as 'generalized servitude', but also overcodes it (*ATP* 457). This can only take place when, on the one hand, workers are no longer slaves, but 'free' to sell their labour-power and, on the other, wealth is no longer linked directly to the money form but becomes 'pure homogeneous and independent capital' (*ATP* 452).

According to Marx, in the *Grundrisse*, this 'freedom' to sell one's labour marks the moment of *alienation* because conscious life-activity becomes converted into alienated labour via capital. Marx argues for a fourfold alienation according to which there is alienation from the *products* of labour, the *processes* of labour, from other workers and from the self – the latter described by him as *Gattungswesen* or 'species-being' (Marx 1973: 496). Once money becomes the generally accepted and standardized equivalent in transactions, everything becomes alienable because anything can be exchanged for money. This is because unlike States that overcode existing symbolic codes and values to engender and reproduce centralized systems of meaning, capitalism does not require beliefs or norms – it simply necessitates an equivalent relation between money and something else, be that a product, an amount of labour-time or a natural resource. *But*, whatever money equates itself to can only be converted into a monetary equivalence once it has been alienated, which itself requires some degree of dispossession. 'Everything is therefore alienable, or indifferent for' and external to the individual, writes Marx (1973: 838). To put it differently, alienation – which is effectuated through primitive accumulation or the appropriation of the means of production – is the organizing mechanism of human activity in the capitalist State, with the result that labour becomes separated from all other productive forces. Once the means of production is appropriated and labour becomes alienated or abstracted, '*surplus labour* appears in objectified form as *surplus product*' and this surplus product – the *commodity* – then valorizes itself as capital (Marx 1973: 450–1). We can see why Marx finds a dialectical relation between productive forces and classes: because the nature of production or labour based on capital is alienating and stratifying. Moreover, this kind of labour relation can only be sustained through force – so work has to become enforced via the State. Clastres, like most anarchists, has a somewhat different take on alienation. He argues that it 'is political before it is economic'; in other words, he thinks alienation precedes capitalism and that it is a product of the State's stratification logics (1989: 198). Society's major division, he opines, is the hierarchical division between the State and the rest of society which forms the base for all other kinds of division, including the division of labour. Moreover, alienation is thought to be central to representation, which is to say that when the State emerged, it established representative mechanisms between it and 'the people', thereby alienating people from their individual and collective capacities to act directly and according to their own needs and desires. Alienation, as a 'social process through which the institutions of social reproduction wrest our creative energy' and 'our capacity to determine the conditions of our existence from us' thus always expresses a 'relationship to domination and exploitation' (Landstreicher 2009: 64).

Just as the State effectuates a logic of enclosure, so too does capitalism and, as with the State, this is a physical enclosure as much as it is one of thought. The anarchist, Alexander Berkman, phrases this well when he asks: 'Did you ever ask yourself how it happens that government and capitalism continue to exist in spite of all the evil and trouble they are causing in the world? If you did, then your answer must have been that it is because the people support those institutions, and that they support them because they *believe* in them' (1972: 223). The generalized belief in the beneficence of the State and capitalism is, therefore, the very thing that maintains private ownership, the concentration of wealth, the hierarchical relationships between different kinds of people and the exploitation of natural resources, to name a few. Yet this belief did not take hold overnight – the abstraction of labour 'took several centuries of brute force and violence on a large scale to literally torture people into the unconditional service of the labour idol' (Krisis Group 2017). It was through prolonged violence that the capitalist State enclosed people's bodies and minds. In the process, capitalism changed *how* and *what* we think through the creation of new, pervasive concepts. *Invest* in your future. Don't *bank* on it. I don't *buy* what you're saying. Time is *money*. Capitalism thus had material effects on our thought processes as is reflected in our language use and, as the latter phrase indicates, also enclosed time as clock time, which is to say, quantified time. 'Neutral' time, where 'minutes of happiness' are treated in exactly the same way 'as minutes of despair' (Holloway 2010: 135), where the past is the present is the future – always task-orientated, always 'external and imposed', always 'an imposition of discipline' (Holloway 2010: 137). Commenting on this disciplining apparatus and aesthetic of capitalism, the anarchist George Woodcock concludes that clock-time, exemplified by clock-in/clock-out systems, is an apparatus of industrial exploitation because 'the clock turns time from a process of nature into a commodity that can be measured and bought and sold' (1977: 132). Time, as clock-time, thus imposes a new regularity which maps out the conditions of possibility in advance.

Alienation and repression

Although Deleuze and Guattari draw on Marx in their theorization of capitalism, they develop their own set of concepts to both extend and critique Marx. Moreover, they aim to situate Marx and capitalist theory within a specific social milieu because their aim is to argue that the individualized psychic repression theorized by Freud as Oedipal repression is actually a nervous condition or psychosis born of social repression – so Oedipal repression is a consequence of capitalism, as we saw in Chapter 1. Psychoanalysis, accordingly, did not invent Oedipus, it merely provided the couch from which to analyze the ascetic ideal and repressive-disciplining elements needed by the capitalist State to thrive. This is where Deleuze and Guattari's analysis is close to anarchist analyses because the problem for them is not so much about needs-based production versus alienated labour as it is about what capitalism has done to processes of subjectivation and by what means such capitalist modes of living have become normalized. To this end, Deleuze and Guattari, in *Anti-Oedipus*, attempt to understand some of the effects that the abstraction of labour – into something that can be exchanged for money – had on desire. Essentially, they bring together Marx's concept of 'labour power' and Freud's concept of 'libido' but rename these *social production* and *desiring-production* respectively. Deleuze and Guattari hold that desire is primary because it constitutes our very life force. This is why they refer to it as 'the production of production' (*AO* 6). Desire, in other words, is a productive force because we use it to produce relations between people, create objects we want and need and so on. For them, desire is neither a structure nor a fantasy, nor a repression, nor the result of lack – and this is where they differ fundamentally with Freud, and indeed with Lacan. For them desire is a flow, but one which is invested, arrested, boosted and directed by other machines in society – be that the State, capitalism, the family, a love interest or ideology. Desire thus has no inherent valence; it can produce positively or negatively; it all depends on how it is machined.

Social production is one of the ways in which desire can become machined – in Deleuze and Guattari's words, it is 'purely and simply desiring-production itself under determinate conditions' (*AO* 29). Differently put, desiring-machines 'are the fundamental category of the economy of desire' as well as the locus of psychic repression, whereas social production is what provokes the psychic repression (*AO* 32). It becomes clearer now to see what Deleuze and Guattari are driving at: they want to understand how desire or life energy becomes invested in the social field and how this investment, in turn, is synthesized to produce certain forms of subjectivity. Moreover, they want to theorize at least some of the ways in which the production of subjectivity changed in capitalist societies – 'to analyze the specific nature of the libidinal investments in the economic and political spheres, and thereby to show how, in the subject who desires, desire can be made to desire its own repression' (*AO* 105). But whereas Marx would make an argument centred on labour alienation, ideology, class stratification and force, Deleuze and Guattari develop a general theory of desire and its relation to the forces of production and anti-production, assemblages of enunciation and power organizations, with all its attendant forms of governmentality of which discipline and control are paradigmatic.

According to Deleuze and Guattari, then, the flows of desire are always assembled – plugged into other flows or machines, interrupting and diverting them just as they will be interrupted and diverted. But when desire is 'plugged into' a capitalist socius – which is not a particular society but a particular instance when the social presents itself as an inscription surface on which all kinds of flows can flow, be interrupted, invested and recorded[3] – several fundamental changes are effectuated, producing deliriums of all kind. Crucially, anti-production is produced by means of immanent syntheses rather than transcendent and overcoding syntheses as is the case with other social machines, such as despotic and imperial States. Anti-production thus 'pervades all production and becomes coextensive with it' (*AO* 250); it 'effuses in the system' and becomes 'loved for itself' (*AO* 346). Simply, 'under the conditions of capital' production becomes loved for the sake of production just as money becomes produced for the sake of more money (*AO* 373). We might even think of anti-production as the mechanism of alienation – the demented, irrational and destructive side of capital production which results variously in effects like Marx's metabolic rift – that irreparable separation between humanity and nature – and Max Stirner's 'spooks', those haunting spectres, such as organized religion or the State, into which we displace reality (Marx 1973: 489; Stirner 1995: 40). Far from being the product of primal repression, as Freud would have it, desire *becomes* repressed. This repression is reinforced through multiple centres of resonance of which the family is only one. With the ascetic ideal fostered in the repressive family as much as through the Church and education, it becomes fully internalized as discipline – a form of governmentality, a strategy and technology that 'traverses every kind of apparatus or institution, linking them, prolonging them, and making them converge and function in a new way' (*F* 25, 26). Following Foucault, Deleuze and Guattari argue that it is discipline – as a site of diffused and heterogeneous power – rather than ideology that produces the ascetic ideal which fundamentally changes the nature of desire in capitalist societies because it *produces* reality in a novel way, thereby creating its own conditions of possibility, long before it 'ideologizes, abstracts or masks' (*F* 29). Moreover, discipline produces original kinds of assemblages of enunciation which, although not a strict mapping, substitute discreet class divisions for Deleuze and Guattari. In any assemblage or desiring-machine, they argue, there are processes of subjectification according to which some subjects are 'subjects of enunciation' (the capitalists) while others are 'subjects of the statement' (the proletarians), though these are never centred on individual or even group agents as it is for Marx who sees individuation as an affair of the subject *qua* class (*ATP* 457). For Deleuze and Guattari, processes of subjectivation are instead semiotic and involve machines of expression that can be either extra-individual in nature – machinic, social, technological, etc. – or infrahuman in nature: 'systems of perception, sensibility, affect, desire', etc. (*MRB* 43). For them, capitalism is thus all about how to connect these disparate flows in the production of subjectivity, how to operate 'in the very hearts of individuals, in their way of perceiving the world, of interacting with the urban fabric, with machinic work processes, and with the social order that supports those productive forces' (*MRB* 36–7). These disparate connections cannot take place solely via alienation and class antagonisms; rather, as anarchists have long argued, class and other antagonisms – such as race, gender and religion, to name a few – are merely the resultants of organizations of power, domination and hierarchy more generally. Hence, large-scale dominations like the State, patriarchy and capitalism are 'the hegemonic effects of a multitude of immediate and minuscule interactions, which continually sustain these dominations and furnish them with the force and intensity that they need in order to reproduce themselves and to pretend to be the origin of their own power' (Colson 2019: 52). In a continuous to and fro, the molecular interactions sustain or perturb the more hegemonic and molar dominations, all of which have an impact on subjective processes – think of the infantilization of women, the racialization of people and the capitalist temporalization of all activities *as well as* the redistributions of these arrangements after 'moments of excess' – a notion we look at more in Chapters 5 and 6. Hence, an analysis of the logics of domination and the resonance between centres of power is more important than an analysis of the interests of a specific category, such as class (Newman 2010b). In this Deleuze and Guattari echo anarchists.

If Marx described concrete assemblages and molar lines of economic stratification, anarchists have always been more interested in understanding the relations between content and expression, the abstract machines and incorporeal transformations effectuated by economic assemblages, where economics is but one facet stemming from a complex relationship between various elements of sociopolitical organization. While Marx predominantly focuses on economics, 'considering the economy the "base" of a society giving rise upon those economic foundations to other social relations', anarchists hold that domination cannot be reduced to economics – 'or even economics *and* political life' (Shannon, Nocella, II and Asimakopoulos 2012: 15). Anarchist principles, analyses and theorizations are, moreover, not limited to 'great men of history'; they are the results of 'collective theorizing by a *libertarian* socialist milieu' (Shannon, Nocella, II and Asimakopoulos 2012: 14). Class, conceived of by Marx as a two-class economic category based on ownership relations and the subjectivation process *par excellence*, is viewed by anarchists as a category that is not reducible to the economic sphere. Bakunin, for example, emphasized a three-class model 'based not only on ownership, but also on the division between mental and manual labor' (Spannos 2012: 47), though most contemporary anarchists would question even a three-class model. Bakunin also predicted the 'Red Bureaucracy' that would arise 'within the Russian Revolution' (Spannos 2012: 48) and described the effects of what Foucault would come to call *disciplinary governmentality*, noting how the 'oppressive conditions' of capitalism 'turn the worker into a subordinate, a passive obedient servant, and the employer into a nearly absolute master' (Bakunin 1926). Kropotkin, for his part, provided an incisive critique of the division of labour encouraged by Adam Smith, also analysed by Marx. Departing from Marx, though, Kropotkin describes the facialization processes of labour division – how 'labelling and stamping' individuals for life destroys 'the love of work and the capacity for invention' (2005: 167). In other words, because people become sorted according to certain logics that predetermine their trajectories, they do not naturally develop their capacities according to what they love doing. This is a freedom largely enjoyed by the privileged. Most people, however, are constrained by the need to work to make a living and have to make do with whatever employment is available for them according to their race, gender, class, education level and country of birth, to name a few facializing factors.

Although Marx insists in his analysis that economic relations are at the root of all relations of domination and subordination, he failed to make any meaningful connection to gendered subjugation. *Mujeres Libres*, Emma Goldman and Voltairine de Cleyre offer important correctives here. It was *Mujeres Libres* who described the 'triple enslavement' of women in terms of them being inferior to men, being subjected to free reproductive labour, and being kept ignorant due to limited education (Ackelsberg 2005: 21). Founded in 1936 by groups of women in Madrid and Barcelona, *Mujeres Libres* 'mobilized over 20,000 women and developed an extensive network of activities designed to empower individual women while building a sense of community' (Ackelsberg 2005: 21). They insisted that freedom be understood as a 'social product' and that women, like men, should be empowered to develop and express their full potential (Ackelsberg 2005: 32, 52). Likewise, Goldman and de Cleyre developed a multi-layered theory of oppression, linking gendered subjugation to the State, the Church, capitalism and patriarchy (Goldman 1996; De Cleyre 2005). Lucy Parsons, a working-class woman of colour and contemporary of Goldman and De Cleyre, also drew attention to the racial dimension of State and capitalist oppression (Parsons 2004). She suffered a severe loss when her husband, the anarchist newspaper editor, Albert Parsons, was executed in connection with the Haymarket massacre, a labour protest at which a bomb killed seven police officers. Due to the public outcry, seven anarchists were accused, including Albert, despite there being no evidence linking them to the bombing. This racial dimension was mobilized to full effect during the colonial years which, in addition to violent conquest, often involved the 'forceful ejection of natives from their lands', laying the foundation for the practically – and actually – wageless workforce needed by early capitalism (Mbah and Igariwey 2001). As colonial governments became replaced, many Global South countries experienced large-scale economic restructuring projects which included 'the introduction of new production processes' and the monetization of the economy (Mbah and Igariwey 2001). This violently transformed longstanding ways of living and being, all but destroying local knowledges and cruelly distorting world views about race – views that continue to circulate, notwithstanding the gains made in many parts of the world. In more recent history, many of these countries have been recolonized through neoliberal strategies that imprison indigenous peoples 'in their *tierras communitarias de origen* (original communal lands)' where they are 'NGOized' as 'essentialist and Orientalist notions become hegemonic, and the indigenous people are turned into multicultural adornment for neoliberalism' (Cusicanqui 2012: 99). In more developed countries, these kinds of conditions were recreated locally as ghettos, shanty towns and other informal or semi-formal settlements. But ghettos 'aren't designed for living. The debris awash in the streets, the broken windows, and the stench of urine in the project elevators and stairwells are the signs of bare life', as Saidiya Hartman reminds us (2006: 88). It is for all these reasons that anarchists, like Deleuze and Guattari, developed more general theories of power, domination and hierarchy, of which the State and capitalism are only two, albeit two important, dimensions. In the next chapter we take a closer look at how such structural domination becomes adopted as a style of life via forms of governmentality, and what some of the consequences have been for contemporary existence.

Tour d'horizon

The first three chapters of this book consider two of the most complex units of analyses in contemporary society, namely the State and capitalism. In the first chapter, I detail one of the major effects the State has had on how we think about social and political organization and, more importantly, what we think is possible in terms of these, which I describe as statist realism – the cognitive-affective distribution that has conditioned people into thinking that life outside of statist societies is impossible. The second chapter takes a closer look at the conditions from which statist realism emerged. Drawing on anarchist and Deleuzoguattarian analyses of the State, I argue that statist realism is grounded in certain foundational axioms which are themselves reliant on the enclosing logics of the State apparatus, effectuated via its apparatus of capture. The aim of this chapter was to denaturalize these widely accepted presuppositions which include the idea that the State is the most advanced and therefore best form of socio-political organization, as well as the idea that the State emerged necessarily instead of contingently. Besides addressing these truisms, I also explained how the State's apparatus of capture works in terms of rent and profit. We saw that to extract rent, the State has to stratify and striate the earth, setting up boundaries for the creation of property. Similarly, to extract profit, the State has to hierarchically divide the social body so that some are forced to work and produce surplus. In this chapter, we looked at the third prong of the apparatus of capture, namely tax, which captures commercial activities by overcoding them, so monetizing the economy. According to Deleuze and Guattari, this changed something at a libidinal level, which is to say that desire became invested in the social field in novel ways which, in turn, engendered entirely novel mechanisms of autonomy and repression, and which expressed radically different forms of subjectivity informed by alienation, the mechanism by which work became divorced from other conscious life-activity.

In their analysis of capitalism, Deleuze and Guattari emphasize the delirium of the capitalist system, observing that it is precisely this irrationality that makes it work well. That is, capitalism thrives on chaos, crisis and change, transforming and updating itself continuously 'insofar as it wards off and repels its own limits' (*ATP* 437). 'This amounts to saying that capitalism forms with a general *axiomatic of decoded flows*', meaning the capitalist system mobilizes mutations and deterritorialized flows by recuperating them for its own ends (*ATP* 453). Because anarchists, like Deleuze and Guattari, recognize that capitalism is not a static system, they have carried forward their critiques of it through notable recent historic movements such as Occupy, anti-austerity movements and the Anti-Globalization Movement. Contrary to dominant narratives that describe globalization in terms of 'increasing interdependence and cooperation through trade' with 'benevolent institutions like the World Bank (WB), the World Trade Organization (WTO), and the International Monetary Fund (IMF)' for overseeing the 'development of so-called Third World nations through capital investment programs', anarchists have critiqued these processes, noting the ways in which these reforms often result in poorer nations steadily becoming poorer, thus becoming ever more dependent on 'already (over)developed nations' (Volcano and Shannon 2012: 81–2). If anything, the structural adjustments implemented by the WB, WTO and IMF through capital investment programmes and as the result of loans usually mean little more than the increased deregulation of poorer economies along with the privatization of their social services.

Over the past two decades or so, capitalism has undergone many more transformations, some of which have been driven by digitization. To be sure, technological advancement has always been a key element in State and capitalist expansion, but recent shifts have prompted new forms of governmentality that we are only just beginning to understand. One of these new forms, namely algorithmic governance – marked by its excess data collection and the development of deep convolutional networks of algorithms which are used variously for 'predictive policing, municipal fee-farming, racialized sub-prime mortgage lending, student debt' and the socialization of marketing through, in large, social media platforms like Facebook, Twitter and Instagram, to name a few – has become the dominant form of governmentality alongside discipline and control, as we see in Chapter 4 (Wark 2020: 94). These new forms of power have altered the socio-political and economic terrains in unprecedented ways. Thinking anarchism after Deleuze and Guattari is productive here precisely because it can help us analyse what is new in our societies. As McKenzie Wark reminds us, it is our task to describe what is emerging rather than what is established. Is this not, after all, what has made the work of Marx, anarchists and Deleuze and Guattari revolutionary? If, however, 'one starts with what is established, it is easy to interpret any new aspect' of the emerging context 'as simply variations on the same essence. Starting with what may be emerging', on the other hand, 'provides a suitable derangement of the senses, a giddy hint that all that was solid is melting into air' (Wark 2019: 42). Chapter 4 thus marks a liminal chapter between the first three and the final two, the latter of which comprise the positive project of the Deleuze-Guattari-anarchism machine. The chapter, while still forming part of the critical-clinical project, takes Deleuze, Guattari and anarchists from behind, as Deleuze would say, because it is, in some ways, a betrayal of them, an infidelity to their work in that I draw on a host of other theorists, but especially Bernard Stiegler, for understanding and further developing an analysis of this new form of governmentality. What comes of this will surely be monstrous but may, if we are lucky, stir the slumber of reason.

4

Hacking for our lives

In 2020 Netflix released a documentary called *The Social Dilemma*, directed by Jeff Orlowski, co-written by him, Davis Coombe and Vickie Curtis. The film, which examines some of the effects suffered by the public due to the unethical methods employed by large tech companies, opens with a quote by Sophocles: 'Nothing vast enters the life of mortals without a curse'. Reminiscent of Paul Virilio's notion of 'the accident', the quote presages the catastrophe immanent to all inventions – certainly all technologies – which is to say that invention '*is merely a way of seeing*', and accidents merely a way of seeing a substance for what it is (Virilio 2005: 5). 'The shipwreck is consequently the futurist invention of the ship, and the air crash the invention of the supersonic airliner, just as the Chernobyl meltdown is the invention of the nuclear power station' (Virilio 2005: 5). Accidents, in other words, happen in advance, long before the actual occurrence, when hubris bites.

The scene thus set, the aims of the documentary become apparent: examining malisons, specifically those unforeseen spillovers from the creations of big tech companies like Apple, Google, Facebook, Twitter and Pinterest. What is not yet obvious is that the accident is *us*. To be sure, the tools created by these companies have had a hugely positive impact, as Tim Kendall, former Director of Monetization at Facebook and former President of Pinterest, explains. Lost family members have been united, organ donors have been found and long-distance friendships have been maintained. But, as these tools developed and spread, they started taking on a contaminant element, announcing their pharmacological attributes – at once curative and poisonous. It is these unpredicted toxic elements that made Kendall and others in the industry, such as Justin Rosenstein – inventor of the Facebook 'like' button – become wary of both the technologies and the companies that run them.

The camera, at this time, moves between the now shifty participants citing their long conversations with lawyers. Clearly, talking about these 'accidents' is not uncomplicated nor, they tell us, does it concern one overriding issue. The problem, it would seem, is multifaceted and includes the concentration of power via data collection and use; the emergence of fake news, misinformation and disinformation which are often spread through hashtags, right-wing mobilization, political polarization, election hacking and the manipulation of public opinion – all of which takes place with unprecedented speed and ease; inscrutable surveillance practices with inimitable economic imperatives; technological overdependence and addiction, and a sharp increase in mental illness, especially in younger generations, counting isolation, depression, ADHD, anxiety and what has been termed 'snapchat dysmorphia' – an obsession with perfect and perfectible appearance, exacerbated by tools on platforms like Snapchat and Instagram which provide filters for feature enhancement. This is not an exhaustive list, and neither are these accidents. The accident is *us*, or more precisely, how we are adapting to these new technologies and being transformed by them.

Initially people who spent most of their free time online and believed that posts carry special import – referred to as 'Extremely Online people' – were limited in number. But, as these technologies spread and became more addictive – in large because that is what they are designed to do – the number of Very Online people increased dramatically, aggravated by the Covid-19 pandemic which has forced many people into online environments for long hours of the day. One of the consequences of this extended online life is that various search engines and social media platforms using algorithms have increasingly been able to adapt what they present to each individual as an impartial view of reality based on how each person interacts with those platforms and others on them. Never before have the decisions of a handful of companies had such a wide impact, and this is precisely what led Tristan Harris – former Google Design Ethicist, and Co-Founder and President of The Center for Humane Technology – to ask: 'Is this normal, or have we fallen under some kind of spell?' A spell that has turned *us* into the products 'for markets trading in human futures', as Professor Emeritus Shoshana Zuboff says in the documentary. That is to say, the new reality we find ourselves in is one where we are being tracked *all the time* by the apps on our phones and computers, producing more information that could ever have been imagined. Powered by algorithms, these apps are designed to keep us addicted, keep us scrolling, keep us clicking. These actions teach the algorithms how to predict our behaviours and prompt our movements and activities from which they 'learn' yet again and improve their predictions, creating a closed loop system that goes from dopamine hit to dopamine deficit state to dopamine hit, on and on and on. What characterizes these technologies is that they have become persuasive, and this lends a certain power to them – a power by which they can modify behaviour in real time. More insidious, though, is that they have disappeared, woven themselves into the fabric of everyday life, becoming indistinguishable from it, always with us, constantly vying for our attention, hacking our very lives – which is why *The Social Experiment* would have been a more apt title: because *we are the experiment.*

We have followed several lines of decoding and deterritorialization: the decoding of the *flows* of production through mercantilism; the deterritorialization of the earth by way of primitive accumulation, which is to say the enclosure of the commons, privatization and the concomitant 'creation' of land; the decoding of the *forces* of production through rent, profit and taxation; the decoding of the *means* of production through surplus value and industrial capital;

the decoding of the worker through surplus labour and machines; the deterritorialization of original affluence through monetary abstraction; and the decoding of States through debt and financial capital (*AO* 225). The latter passage of flux – alternatively referred to as neoliberalism, globalization or corporate capitalism – has rendered everyone a mini-corporation, organized around the 'relationship of investor and executive', characterized by branding and outsourcing – corporate speak for the marketization of individuals, the casualization of work and the precarization of workers (Graeber 2011: 377).[1] 'Each passage of a flux is a deterritorialization, and each displaced limit, a decoding' – yes, capitalism 'schizophrenizes more and more on the periphery' (*AO* 232). And yet, Deleuze and Guattari remind us, this is nothing more than a universal history of *contingency* (*AO* 224). *And yet*, if there is anything we have learnt by now it is that capitalism is a resilient system, 'oftentimes changing features in reaction to class struggle as well as to its own limitations. As opponents of capitalism, then, anarchists have been concerned not just with describing capitalism as it is, but also capitalism as it *may be*' (Shannon, Nocella II and Asimakopoulos 2012: 16). This means updating our analyses and forsaking fetishized theories that have become the limits of our own thinking – our own little Oedipuses, our own dogmatic images of thought.

Modulation in societies of hyper-control

What capitalism *may be* is what Deleuze described as societies of control shortly before his death. Grappling with the convergence of cybernetics and capitalism, he theorized that we have moved from Foucault's disciplinary societies, characterized by enclosed spaces that operate according to a logic of moulding – the school, the university, the factory – to societies of control, where the logics is that of modulation, 'states of perpetual metastability', according to which nothing is ever finished (1992b: 4). Instead of moving from one enclosed space to another after having achieved a predetermined goal – symbolized by the high-school certificate, the university degree, the work promotion – there is a continual adaptation to shifting criteria. But modulation is not used consistently in Deleuze's oeuvre. In *Difference and Repetition*, for example, Deleuze draws on philosopher Gilbert Simondon's use of the concept to 'resist the idea of moulding, which has been central to Western ideas of the relationship between form and materiality at least since Aristotle', and which is paradigmatic of hylomorphism that 'understands being in terms of form and matter, conceived as absolutely distinct categories' (Hui 2015a: 76). Modulation, here, is therefore understood as an intensive variation or flux in a metastable, rather than homeostatic, system. Drawing on thermodynamics, Simondon, like Deleuze, understands the 'structure' of the individual not in ontological terms but in ontogenetic terms as a phase shift between two *disparate* states. Modulation is a response to this *disparation* or tension, where the disparateness forms the primer for *individuation*, a partial and relative resolution to a prior tension rather than a dialectic operation as is the case with hylomorphism which is conceived as 'form+matter=synthesis' (Hui 2015a: 77; see also Simondon 2009: 10 and *DR* 246). Modulation, in the sense that it is used in *Difference and Repetition*, thus has a positive valence because it gives us information about how ontogenesis works and how it can give rise to genuinely novel forms of thought and experience. In the 'Postscript on the Societies of Control', however, modulation takes on a negative valence in reference to its digitized form because Deleuze, in this text, is theorizing how ontogenetic processes or individuation become short-circuited – and it is precisely this short-circuiting of individuation processes that Bernard Stiegler argues has become characteristic of what he refers to as societies of *hyper*-control.[2]

Although this eclipsing or short-circuiting is theorized in far more detail by Stiegler, it is already described to some extent by Deleuze in his

Postscript where he details the decoding of the code from watchwords in disciplinary societies to passwords in control societies, and the deterritorialization of the individual into the 'dividual', comprised of collections or 'banks' of data, statistics, samples and so on (1992b: 5). Deleuze calls this the 'capitalism of higher-order production' to emphasize the shift from the factory to the corporation, the latter of which no longer has the ideals and methods of mercantile or industrial capital. Neither is it concerned with buying raw materials and selling finished products or commodities. What it wants to sell, instead, 'is services and what it wants to buy is stocks. This is no longer a capitalism for production but for the product, which is to say, for being sold or marketed' (1992b: 6). This corporatization is what eventually leads to the complete transformation of the commodity into the *derivative* – 'a form of information through which each of the component flows in commodification can be subdivided, valued, combined, and sold again as financial instruments' (Wark 2020: 72). This transformation, as Deleuze already observed, also affects the individual, now the dividual or aggregate data set – a derivative – which Randy Martin calls the new 'unit of wealth' in financialized capital where we see a 'shift in policy emphasis from providing security to managing risk' (2015: 60, 55). This modification became profoundly pronounced after the 2008 crash when Alan Greenspan, former chairman of the Federal Reserve, 'saved' capitalism by advancing neoliberalism, thereby 'expanding "free" trade, deregulating markets and economies by removing government oversight, and privatizing everything from water to schools and parks, as a process aimed at reversing Keynesian economic policy' (Volcano and Shannon 2012: 84).

Since then, neoliberalism has itself undergone a subtle mutation so that if the conundrum was how to manage risk in control societies, it has, in societies of hyper-control, become how to manage risk in an open environment at any given moment. Guattari even imagined a city where one would be tracked continuously 'thanks to one's (dividual) electronic card' linked to a 'computer that tracks each person's position – licit or illicit – and effects a universal modulation' (Deleuze 1992b: 7). How prescient these visions were, even though neither Deleuze nor Guattari could foreknow the full scope of what has become known alternatively as cognitive capitalism (Yann Moulier-Boutang 2012), the age of planetary computerization (Guattari 2013), algorithmic governmentality (Rouvroy and Berns 2013), The Stack (Bratton 2015), platform capitalism (Srnicek 2016), infopolitics (Koopman 2018), surveillance capitalism (Zuboff 2019), computational capitalism (Stiegler 2019) and the cybernetic episteme (Tiqqun 2020). The reason is simple: what would become the societies of hyper-control in which algorithmic reason governs was still emerging. Who could have possibly foreseen what the cybernetic dream – the brainchild of Norbert Wiener and his milieu, ultimately concerned with *'the practical problem of mastering uncertainty'* – would become and how it would provoke a veritable redistribution of the partitioning of the sensible? (Tiqqun 2020: 38). For if Wiener wanted nothing less than to translate risk and uncertainty into *information* and to control this information via a circular causality, recursion,[3] he did not yet have the means to do so. The full emergence of algorithmic governance would only take place in our recent history, with the convergence of five major developments: a profusion of *data* gathered from and produced by embedded sensors and platforms like social media; deep convolutional networks of *algorithms* comprising multiple interconnected layers that can sift through the deluge of raw data through specific types of analyses such as pattern recognition; *networks* that make possible the immediate, cost-effective and pervasive transmission of data and their analyses; capacious and flexible storage via the *cloud* – 'the governing nexus' or *nomos* of information (Bratton 2015: 111); and advances in *hardware* that 'have added sheer power to the capture and analysis of data' (Kalpokas 2019: 2–3).

It was from this convergence, then, that the cybernetic episteme emerged, offering a 'political solution' to 'the becoming-ungovernable of the world's labor forces and populations' as opposed to 'a purely technical one' (Tiqqun 2020: 9) – its mega-infrastructure leaving behind a carbon footprint of digital waste that Benjamin Bratton describes as 'perhaps the hungriest thing in the world' (2015: 94). This new episteme is characterized by hyper-control, which is to say by digitized modulation – a type of modulation marked by recursive regulation or feedback loops that prompt continual adaptation not only to 'the working principle of computation' but to a new way of *thinking* that 'extends beyond computers to social and economic modeling' (Hui 2018: 147). That is, algorithmic reason has melded with our own cognitive structures. A new micropolitics, then, a new abstract machine diagramming the field of possibility so that the problem of cybernetics is no longer restricted to that of '*forecasting the future but reproducing the present*' – collapsing metastable systems into homeostatic ones through a heady 'mix of *surveillance and capture* apparatuses' (Tiqqun 2020: 56, 70). In effect, the socialization of these apparatuses provides a new rhythm of calculability to the fluxes of control. These new legibility practices have allowed markets to 'see' us in an entirely new way, all the while teaching us 'to see ourselves in that way, too': abstractly, derivatively, algorithmically – the entirety of life financialized or, what comes to the same, probabilized (Fourcade and Healy 2017: 10). Meanwhile, the technologies have all but disappeared, woven as they are 'into the fabric of everyday life', becoming 'indistinguishable from it' (Weiser 1991: 95).

Information, data and hacking

The question that arises is how to conceptualize subjectivation processes when information – individuals *as* information – has become a form of monopolized property? Wark proposes that we re-envision Marx's understanding of class to account for information not so much in terms of 'a quantity of surplus value' as an exploitation of the 'asymmetry of information' from which certain classes derive power (Wark 2019: 54). They suggest, accordingly, a distinction between what they call the 'vectoralist' classes and the 'hacker classes', where the difference between these resides in their relation to information – not only information as digitized data, but any information. The point is that once information becomes proprietary it 'becomes the basis of a form of accumulation in its own right' (Wark 2004: 82). Whereas the locus of power in capitalism lies in the means of production, that is no longer solely the case because information now functions in a similar way as the means of production used to. The vectoralist classes are thus so named because 'they control the vectors along which information is abstracted' – be that property vectors or derivatives vectors (Wark 2004: 11). Hacker classes, on the other hand, express knowledge rather than controlling the vectors of information. They make abstractions as much as they are made abstract (Wark 2004: 3). In the same way as land is an abstraction of the earth and capital an abstraction of resources, as we saw in Chapters 2 and 3, so too information is an abstraction derived from the hack. The power of the vectoralist classes lies in 'the accumulation of interest, which in this context means not just the return on the investment of information in the form of money but any surplus information, acquired through unequal exchanges of information' – like the information Google, Apple, Facebook and Twitter have of us which they use to predict and shape our behaviour (Wark 2015). This is what Shoshana Zuboff calls 'surveillance capitalism' – a new instantiation of capitalism which 'operates through unprecedented asymmetries in knowledge and the power that accrues to knowledge' so that surveillance capitalists, or the vectoralist classes, 'know everything about us' while 'their operations are designed to be unknowable to us' (Zuboff 2019: 11). Hackers, unlike the vectoralists, are producers but they do not own what they produce – they are dispossessed at the level of the individual and the level of a class, just as the proletarians conceived of by Marx were. The vectoralists classes, on the other hand, own and monopolize the vectors of information, feverishly accumulating and stockpiling data via information dragnets which categorize and position people according to risk and worth. Hacking is not 'bad' per se though – it is productive *and* destructive, just as information is at once resistance *and* that which it resists: 'its own dead form, communication' (Wark 2004: 56) which recoils the 'subject of the enunciation' into a 'subject of the statement' (*ATP* 159).

If you have a social media profile, if you access the internet, if you have a smart phone, you are hacking. In this sense, hacking is the new productive synthesis, the new production of production – concurrently producing mechanisms for inscription *and* an apparatus of repression. Positively, hacking is 'inherently connective in nature' and constitutes a desirous coupling, a continuous plugging into other flows that causes currents to flow and break (*AO* 5). But in the digital milieu these are incomplete inscriptions, and it is precisely this partial transference which produces an apparatus of repression. Moreover, this new kind of information has little if anything to do with meaning; it is, rather, 'a ratio of novelty and redundancy' (Wark 2020: 210). The digital and automated 'inscription' that takes place is, consequently, that of a closed commercial loop where the aim is the production of an optimized market *of one*, exemplified by the individualized experiences produced by the algorithmic processes deployed by large tech companies like Facebook and Amazon. Hackers are not passive bystanders, however; they are actively selecting information, producing novelty and redundancies, curating and being curated, personalizing and being personalized, emerging, *becoming* all the while, though it is a becoming informed and shaped by algorithmic intervention. Algorithms, then, are not mere codes; they are ethico-political arrangements of values, assumptions and propositions about the world, operating according to a distinctive power that Colin Koopman calls *infopower*, which he distinguishes from Foucault's biopower and anatomopower. That is, he sees infopower as a new regularity that diagrams the conditions of possibility. Whereas anatomopolitics (discipline) is concerned with normalization and biopolitics with a regulatory power operating at the biological level of a population mass according to distinctive techniques that include statistics, demography and so on, infopolitics concerns data or, more specifically, the 'formats through which data fasten us' to 'a data point' and augment 'the velocity with which we can be handled as a data point' (Koopman 2018: 117, 106).

Algorithmic governmentality and reticulated subjectivation

Legal theorist, Antoinette Rouvroy, understands the management of individuals-as-data as a bypassing of 'subjectivity by automation' so that the subject is reduced to a 'collection of infra-individual data' that are 'recomposed at a supra-individual level under the form of a profile' in a kind of pure immanent totality – 'a world liberated from contingency and unpredictability' (Rouvroy and Stiegler 2016: 11, 12; Rouvroy 2011: 130). This ever-increasing governance of the 'real' is what she calls *algorithmic governmentality*, following Foucault's understanding of governmentality as the 'conduct of conduct' (Rouvroy 2011: 119; Foucault 2008: 186). If legitimacy and authority for the State were vested in the image of savagery, and for capitalism in the invisible hand, it is, for algorithmic governmentality, vested in uncertainty, specifically the hedging of risk associated with uncertainty. Derivatives – and the derivatization of data – present one such way 'to hedge risk and extract a return from an unknowable future by hedging its various possibilities' via a recursive logic that prices uncertainty (Wark 2020: 82). *We have all become that risk. We have all become derivatives.* Fragmented subjects: an unknowable from which returns are extracted, the 'anticipation of catastrophe' now 'a design principle: "Design for failure, since everything fails" is a well-known slogan of Amazon's cloud computing' (Hui 2015b: 125). This form of governmentality, argues Zuboff, became fast-tracked by the 2008 crash and 9/11 before that which legitimized a kind of continual 'state of exception'. Zuboff, accordingly, describes 9/11 as a 'historical condition that lent shelter to the fledgling market form' that would become what she names *surveillance capitalism*. As Koopman and Rouvroy, Zuboff recognizes a new form of power which she terms *instrumentarianism*, so defined because of 'the instrumentation and instrumentalization of behavior for the purposes of modification, prediction, monetization, and control' (Zuboff 2019: 352). It is a milieu marked by ambient connectivity and data harvesting in which we have become 'leaky bodies', our data characteristics imperceptible to ourselves, even though we are hyper-visible and encouraged to reveal ourselves as much as possible, 'only for the revealed attributes and traits to be used to gently and pleasurably nudge us in predefined directions' (Kalpokas 2019: 16, 17). Yes, being a hacker is pleasurable, becoming data is pleasurable too. Libidinal economy stems, after all, from the binding and unbinding of drives – and this is where Stiegler's work provides an important segue into Deleuze and Guattari's because he makes a useful distinction between desire and the drives, as we see in Chapter 5. Extending what Deleuze began to theorize in his Postscript, Stiegler understands marketing as *the* instrument 'systemically and systematically' producing 'the exasperation of the drives', even if it *feels* good to some extent, perhaps for that very reason (2019: 177). If libidinal economy is that which 'transforms the drives necessarily contained in each of us into social energy invested in a thousand ways, through the most ordinary dreams as well as the wildest ones' then it is necessary to understand the conditions of their production – which Stiegler does in terms of what he calls *grammatization* and *proletarianization* (2019: 184).

Properly speaking, individuals are technical beings straight away because memory and knowledge are 'originally exteriorized' – at least partially and mnemotechnically, whether via tools and artefacts or social formations, organizations and rituals (Stiegler 2006). Such exteriorized memory, also known as *hypomnesis*, frees *anamnesis* or functional memory from its overall dependence on the human mind by becoming located in a *technical object*, the form of exteriorization. This takes place via certain logics and techniques, or *technē*, for example orthographic grammatization which extends oral technologies through writing, printing and painting. The point is that grammatization constitutes a 'relationship between understanding, reason, imagination and intuition that comes to be transformed' (Stiegler 2019: 240). In its positive iteration, this transformation aids intergenerational and transgenerational memory and relations for the production of long circuits which are needed for the 'passage of thought across time' as well as the construction of collective futural projection and action (Stiegler and Rogoff 2010). In its negative iteration, this externalization is transformed into something that *disrupts* the production of long circuits. This disruption has been accelerated in societies of hyper-control due to the virtually continuous connection we have with mnemotechnological devices and the near-automatic 'dumping' of memory into these devices – cell phones being paradigmatic. These new hypomnesic systems have transformed hypomnesis into storage where externalized memory is kept without being used. According to Stiegler this has initiated a '*structural loss* of memory', a disruption of *all* forms of knowledge – and it is precisely this disruption that he conceives of as a *generalized proletarianization* – the loss of work-knowledge (*savoir-faire*), life-knowledge (*savoir-vivre*) and conceptual knowledge (Stiegler 2006;

2019: 14). Together, grammatization and proletarianization contract processes of individuation, which is to say that the practically ubiquitous deployment of algorithmic processes and infrastructures short-circuit our psychic, individual and collective protentions – or the way in which we anticipate the future through our individual and collective will, desires and expectations – systemically and systematically replacing them with algorithmically generated or digital tertiary retentions and protentions (Stiegler 2018: 96). This shift is not merely technical for Stiegler, meaning a transition from analogue to digital. Rather, he understands it as *organological*, as a question of life and the living subject, where the biological has become technical, organized by the organic as much as the inorganic. To theorize this shift, Stiegler develops a number of concepts that are pertinent for thinking our current situation in conjunction with Deleuze, Guattari and anarchism, of which only a few will be expounded here.

Stiegler's theorization of tertiary – and digital tertiary – retentions and protentions are grounded in the time-consciousness theory of Husserl, who conceives of the manner in which we experience and synthesize ourselves in time in terms of a first level, where *primary* protention and retention occur – a binding process that categorizes incoming stimuli and information – and a second level where recollection and vaticination transpire, which Stiegler renames *secondary* retention and protention. For Husserl we gain our *time-consciousness* when the primal impression of the present moment is retained as the immediate past of *retention*, which allows for an unfolding of the anticipated future of *protention*. These three non-discreet instances are bound together in a single aggregative process of duration (Husserl 1991: 21–8). Whereas primary retentions are related to binding, secondary retentions 'are of the past, they are things you have formerly experienced' which informs what is experienced in the present – so secondary retentions can be said to partially and contingently condition or 'determine primary retentions' (Rouvroy and Stiegler 2016: 20). Put differently, primary retention is 'the material of perception, and therefore of the present inasmuch as it presents itself, which is to say that the present is a dynamic process of presentation' and selection, whereas secondary retention is basically the memory 'of the past, of what is absent and represented by a dynamic process of imagination' (Stiegler 2019: 215). Tertiary retentions and protentions, in contrast, constitute the array of spatiotemporal connective material or *hypomnemata* – externalized memory – that serves as the conduits for the passage of collective thought which, along with secondary retention and protention, or functional memory, informs and contingently structures primary retention and protention, all of which take place via continual processes of individuation and transindividuation.

Like many of his concepts, Stiegler adopts individuation and transindividuation from Simondon to philosophically explain the passaging of life as recurrent phase-shifts, but whereas individuation refers to a partial and relative resolution to a prior tension in the individual, *transindividuation* – as the term implies – resides *between* the 'I' and the 'we' in a procedure of co-individuation, transforming both 'through one another' (Stiegler and Rogoff 2010). Transindividuation is thus 'an activity of the psychosocial side of memory' which facilitates the construction of long circuits (Stiegler 2006). However, digitized retentions and protentions have attenuated these processes in unparalleled ways, especially because the speed at which they function modulates behaviour in real time, leading to grammatization and proletarianization. Whereas protentions are generally 'transindividuated and transformed into a common rule, that is, into habits and conventions of all kinds, metastabilized between the psychic individuals and the collective individuals associated with these experiences', there occurs in algorithmic societies a hyper-synchronization of individual and collective life (Stiegler 2016: 140). Stiegler calls this *hyper-diachronization* to connote processes of disindividuation, or the inability to individuate, due to a short-circuiting or premature interruption of processes of subjectivation and a concomitant disruption in the creation of long circuits. Instead, there is a conversion of individuation into individual*ization* – a new kind of stratification that divides the individual at the infra-level, unbinding the drives through an automatization that reticulates noetic life, inducing a loss of reason, and reasons for living and dreaming. The consequences are devastating: an inability to produce shared horizons and social practices of collective meaning that carry across the passage of time, pre- and overdetermined as they are by digital tertiary retentions and protentions.

This leads Stiegler, in *The Age of Disruption*, to describe our contemporary era as '*the epoch of the absence of epoch*', by which he means 'the epoch of reticulated and automated disruption' (2019: 5, 8). Marked by an overexposure to digital and automated technologies, and a generalized reflexive impotence triggered by the knowledge of impending ecological collapse, the future is contracted into a negative collective protention. For Stiegler, then, desire is *disrupted* or short-circuited, rather than schizophrenized as it was for Deleuze and Guattari, because the transmission of inter- and transgenerational knowledge, which includes a common horizon of future expectations, is precluded. To compensate for this lack of collective secondary protention, tertiary protention – an artificial process – becomes the *default*, functioning as a *pharmakon*, curative and poisonous at once, because it constitutes an amelioration for what has been lost while, at the same time, inflecting and accelerating that loss. One of the consequences is 'abject aboulia' – a disaffected withdrawal that marks a new instantiation of alienation (Stiegler 2019: 20). This alienation is, as we have seen, the result of the immense modification of processes by which collective secondary retentions are interiorized because they have become replaced by digital and automated systems that have themselves become the material for circuits of transindividuation, though these are reticulated transindividuations. In other words, the automatic protentions that arise from these reticulated retentions eclipse processes of individuation and transindividuation, replacing them with processes of dividuation and transdividuation, individualization and transindividualization. This hyper-individualism is sustained through short-circuits which radically alter the synthesis and metastabilization of our time-consciousness because they disrupt the production of consistency which is partly achieved through long circuits or knowledge that is passed on over time and across space and which, more importantly, conditions the horizon of future expectation, which is to say collective protentions. Disrupted, we produce not reason but deliriums of all kinds. Whereas transindividuation is the '*becoming reasonable* of what will initially have been mad' through processes of, for example, transvaluation, disruption is the process *par excellence* of market-driven exosomatization, the becoming algorithmic of reason (Stiegler 2019: 93). 'Reason finds itself systemically short-circuited', writes Stiegler. '*The reality of disruption is the loss of reason*' and the 'perfect completion of nihilism' (2019: 38). This gives rise to an anoetic living species with a form of interiority bereft of individuation and transindividuation processes, a form of interiority that is always-already 'dreaming the next stage of its self-exosomatization' (Stiegler 2019: 110).

Pharmacology, symptomatology, ecosophy and social ecology

If it all seems rather bleak, the good news is that for Stiegler, as for Deleuze and Guattari and Nietzsche before them, health is not opposed to illness. They are, rather, immanent to each other. For Stiegler, the pharmacological situation is a transitional period during which we encounter the *pharmakon* – that which is both a remedy and a poison at the same time. What determines which of these immanent conditions becomes amplified depends on our attention to and care of it. Here it becomes obvious why the algorithmic and ecological *pharmaka* have become destructive: because of a lack of attention and care, by which Stiegler means a 'rational form of care' that maintains reason through the 'formation and training of deep attention' aimed at the production of long circuits (2013a: 22). In Chapter 5, we take a closer look at pharmacology. For now, it suffices to say that it resonates with Deleuze's notion of symptomatology and Guattari's concept of ecosophy.

Drawing on Nietzsche, who first thought of philosophers and artists as clinicians of culture, Deleuze develops the idea of symptomatology in his work, beginning with an extensive exposition of it in *Masochism: Coldness and Cruelty* (1991c). What interests Deleuze is not symptomatology per se, but what symptomatology allows for: a fabulative therapy or positive task. Deleuze's symptomatology should thus be viewed as a triadic method consisting of a diagnosis, the formulation of problems and fabulation. The first part is straightforward enough – it involves the description of a set of symptoms. Deleuze tells us that medicine 'distinguishes between syndromes and symptoms, a symptom being the specific sign of an illness, and a syndrome the meeting-place or crossing-point of manifestations issuing from very different origins and arising within variable contexts' (*M* 13–14). Both aspects are important for Deleuze: not merely describing a set of symptoms but also understanding symptoms contextually and as a practice of art, not dialectics. 'In place of a dialectic which all too readily perceives the link between opposites, we should aim for a critical and clinical appraisal able to reveal the truly differential mechanisms as well as the artistic originalities', writes Deleuze (*M* 14). This is where the second aspect – the problem or *problématique* – comes in which Deleuze, drawing on Simondon, relates to disparateness, the primer for individuation. Disparateness, which involves 'at least two orders of magnitude or two scales of heterogeneous reality between which potentials are distributed' is the primer for the unfolding or opening of a 'problematic field' which is 'determined by the distance between two heterogeneous orders' (*DR* 246). What should have become clear in this chapter is at least some of the ways in which the problematic field has been redistributed by algorithmic processes and how disparation is contracted, narrowing the field of possibility within which partial and relative solutions are generated through processes of individuation and transindividuation. Understanding how such reticulation works in algorithmic societies forms the basis of a diagnosis which reveals to us a disconnect between short circuits and long circuits and, thus, the absence of collective dreaming in the face of absolute nihilism. This, then, is the task of fabulation which comprises the co-constitutive action of invention *and* therapy, specifically the invention of a missing people and the application of the therapeutic method which Deleuze and Guattari name *schizoanalysis* in *Anti-Oedipus* as we see in Chapter 6.

A similar holistic method is evident in Guattari's ecosophical approach, best understood as an ethico-political articulation between three ecological registers – environmental ecology, social ecology and mental ecology. Like Stiegler, Guattari grapples in *The Three Ecologies* (2000) with changes in subjectivity that have come about due to unprecedented scientific and technological advances which, for him, has effectuated an ecological disequilibrium – in nature, in the psyche and in society at large. Ecosophy is thus aimed at thinking about how to produce new forms of valorization grounded in dissensus and resingularization rather than capitalist values, the aim of which is to heal the various forms of alienation in and between people, communities and the environment. For Guattari, the only true response to any of these issues is one that deals with all three registers at the same time, and which is not 'exclusively concerned with visible relations of force on a grand scale', but also takes 'into account molecular domains of sensibility, intelligence and desire' (*TE* 28). In other words, Guattari thinks the way in which we organize at the macro-level is as important as our organization, practices, thoughts and relationships at the micro-level – and in this he echoes anarchists, especially Murray Bookchin who develops a theory of *social ecology* that resonates with Guattari's work on ecosophy. For Bookchin, like Guattari, the ecological and social crises are implicated in mental ecology, which Bookchin describes as an 'underlying mentality of domination' used by humans to retrospectively justify individualism, hierarchical organization, dualistic simplifications and the 'deployment of technology primarily for purposes of social control' (1987: 50, 71). Social ecology is thus Bookchin's response to these interrelated crises – a holistic set of practices that 'challenges the entire system of domination itself and seeks to eliminate the hierarchical and class edifice that has imposed itself on humanity and defined the relationship between nonhuman and human nature' (Bookchin 1993). It is, as such, an ethical responsiveness to the many dimensions of life, aimed at wholeness and future well-being through the creation of what Stiegler would call long circuits.

As mentioned at the end of Chapter 2, these ideas have been taken up and implemented by the Kurdish Freedom Movement in Rojava which emphasizes that solutions to the ecological crisis cannot be left to States, nor relegated to 'science and technology alone' (Internationalist Commune of Rojava 2018: 28). Instead, they practice direct action aimed at building a social-ecological society. Ravished by years of institutionalized and centralized monoculture farming with a strong focus on wheat (think back to Chapter 2 and Scott's ideas about wheat and State expansion), as well as repressive policies that forbade the planting of trees and growing of vegetables, along with the invasion by ISIS and the Turkish occupation of Northern Kurdistan that provoked extensive economic sanctions, the Internationalist Commune of Rojava turned to social ecology which they see as 'the science of people's relationship with their natural and social environments' (Internationalist Commune of Rojava 2018: 42). Creating balance means, for them, the construction of a new social order *and* new social relations based on 'radically democratic structures' outside of State organization and whose decisions take into consideration the impact of 'technologies, modes of production, distribution, and forms of consumption' on the natural environment (Internationalist Commune of Rojava 2018: 45). By paying attention to and taking care of their ecologies they have started a process of *making reasonable* that which was initially mad and have, in the process, produced collective protentions that have engendered reasons for living. Although drawing on Bookchin for theoretical support, the Internationalist Commune underscores that this is not a 'purely descriptive theory', but a practical project aimed at disrupting dogmatic images of thought and so radically altering *how* transformation can be imagined and enacted (Internationalist Commune of Rojava 2018: 42–3). As part of their social-ecological work, the self-governing communes and local populations of Rojava aim to collectivize their land, water and energy, concurrently focusing on self-sufficiency and cooperatives that are 'able to produce according to people's needs' without being trapped by a logic of constant expansion and 'profit maximization' (Internationalist Commune of Rojava 2018: 90–1). This is achieved through, for example, education programmes, waste and water management programmes, the banning of hunting, fishing and farming in newly created nature reserves, reforestation and tree planting activities, food gardens and diversified agriculture and recycling. What is striking is that all these activities and programmes are grounded in values of 'self-help, self-responsibility', radical horizontalized democracy outside of State structures, 'equality, equity and solidarity' (Internationalist Commune of Rojava 2018: 117). In this way, the Internationalist

Commune actively – individually and collectively – produces new forms of valorization grounded in dissensus and resingularization through 'the liberation of singularities that' have been repressed by more 'dominant and dominating' subjectivities, such as those promoted, enforced and normalized by the State, capitalism and the media (*TE* 12). In effect, the Internationalist Commune is hacking back, *hacking for their lives* – not in the neoliberal sense of a 'life hack' or a shortcut that increases productivity and efficiency – but in the sense of a community-operated hackerspace that emphasizes a do-it-yourself ethos and 'open-source' practices, offering a space that is open to everyone who is willing to learn *and* contribute to the community in return.

Tour d'horizon

How do we dream again? How do make life worth living again? These are, for Stiegler, some of *the* questions of our times, deeply tied to the problem of producing long circuits of transindividuation which, as we saw in this chapter, have become short-circuited by digital and automated processes – 'persuasive' technologies that compel and modify our behaviours, often without us even noticing. But these technologies are not only transforming our social interactions – they are changing the very nature of thought through an exosomatization 'that leads to unreason in all its forms', as is evidenced by the proliferation of fake news, populism, conspiracy theories and other kinds of misinformation and disinformation (Stiegler 2019: 101). Designed to be opaque to us, these new technologies continuously collect sensitive information – surplus data produced by us, the hackers. In a cruel twist, we have become the experiment, *we have become the product*. In an even crueler twist, these technologies keep us distracted from real-world problems, one of which is the ecological crisis. To be fair, thinking about Anthropogenic doom is not pleasurable. It does not offer an infinite scroll with a recommended feed. There is nothing to 'like' and 'heart'. And yet, despite collapsing, it is our world – the only one we have, bar narcissistic visions of space colonization – so we have to find ways to believe in it again.

For Stiegler, as we have seen, this has to do with the problem of producing long circuits which bind the drives and transform them into practices of *care*. For anarchists, positive collective protention is also connected to care which they practice and theorize in terms of utopianism, prefiguration and revolution. Similarly, for Deleuze and Guattari, this is about striking a balance between *careful* experimentation and consistency, concepts they discuss from a number of perspectives – such as the three syntheses of time, the Body without Organs, the virtual or plane of consistency, becoming, the ritornello and schizoanalysis – as we see in the next two chapters. This, then, marks the turn of this book because the emphasis is no longer on diagnoses, but on the posing of problems and fabulation, which is to say outlining a positive project synthesizing Deleuze, Guattari and anarchism. This entails thinking about 'the machinic conversion of primal repression' and 'undoing the blockage' on which the repression properly speaking relies by transvaluating what is 'ill' in order to produce healthier intensities, thereby 'causing the desiring-machines to start up again' (*AO* 339). In other words, the next two chapters are aimed at provoking new dreams and reasons for living.

To believe in this world again

In the second season of *Black Mirror*, in an episode titled 'Be Right Back', viewers follow the story of Martha (Hayley Atwell) whose boyfriend, Ash (Domhnall Gleeson), is killed in a car accident. Martha, who meantime discovers that she is pregnant, struggles to come to terms with her new situation. Recognizing her friend's anguish, Sarah (Sinead Matthews) steps in to help Martha by introducing her to a new technology: an online service dealing in digital immortality. This technology uses a person's digital archive – images, social media posts, voice data, text messages and so on – to train chatbots or digital avatars to behave, respond and think like the deceased person. Ostensibly the service exists to help people obtain closure by allowing them to communicate with their loved ones via this artificial intelligence, but instead of helping Martha come to a place of acceptance she realizes, in the twist, that the technology has trapped her in the past, which is to say she grasps that the android is not really Ash and that she has, in essence, been deceiving herself all along.

Great lesson from *Black Mirror*, except it assumes that offline life is what people still primarily want, and that this kind of immersive form of cyber-individuation is rather more reserved for so-called 'Extremely Online people' who struggle more with complex emotions, such as those associated with losing a loved one, due – at least in part – to an overexposure to short-term neurochemical (dopamine) 'hits' related to the expression of simplified emotional responses presented for selection through, for example, emoticons. These default online states, which express a limited range of coded emotions – happy face, sad face, angry face – do not leave much room for the expression of complex affective states and become, more inimically, transferred to real-world interactions where the tendency becomes to reduce nuanced affective positions to internalized emoticons. This kind of arrested emotional development associated with Very Online people is, however, far more prevalent than one might imagine – think about how many times a day you give in to automated preselections, be that in an email or choosing an emoticon. Nevertheless, we do not quite yet live in the world of *Black Mirror*, though we are certainly close. If Martha's scenario seems futuristically realistic, but only *futuristically* so, it may surprise some readers that there is already a similar app in existence. Meet Replika (https://replika.ai/), the AI companion who 'cares', the bot with whom people have real emotional experiences, where you can explore your own personality with a companion who is also *you*.[1] (Be warned, though, the real aim of this app is not to be your friend, but to entice you enough to upgrade to the paid options with sexual content.)

So what is the problem? Dreams of life amongst androids are nothing new, though there has perhaps been a subtle shift of emphasis from service robots to social robots over the past two decades. There is even a field of study called Lovotics, aimed at creating reciprocal love connections between human beings and robots. And anyway, who is to say remote mediated human communication isn't beneficial?

In *What Makes Life Worth Living*, Stiegler explains the assimilation of new life experiences in terms of *adoption* – the transitional period during which we encounter the *pharmakon* or pharmacological situation that is at once destructive and curative. Precisely which immanent conditions are affirmed and become amplified depends on our ability to *attentively* carve some consistency out of the 'chaos' that the new situation presents, part of which comprises the creation of novel relations. Martha, having learnt of Ash's death, faces this pharmacological situation – one which forces her to confront the question: *Is life worth living?* In her melancholy she is unable to pay attention to the fact that the *pharmakon* is the condition of its own critique and that overcoming its destructive trajectories necessitates processes of individuation and transindividuation – the production of consistency or, more accurately, metastability, that allows for a certain amount of experimentation or, in Martha's case, simply enough life force to circulate new intensities so that the transitional event can be adopted or reconstructed and given new meaning so that life can feel worth living again (Stiegler 2013a: 16). But, because Martha wants to avoid feeling the pain of loss, she fails to pay attention to and take care of the *pharmakon*, so short-circuiting her processes of individuation and transindividuation, effectively trapping herself in a kind of bardo, a state of intermediate existence, *limbo*. She has *adapted* to her situation through a reticulated retention – a transindividuation process formed through short circuits. In so doing, she also traps the intensities that *exceed* her current situation because she has denied herself the pharmacological moment: the wound which, if it were allowed to affect her very being, would become her healing. But being affected – rather than disaffected – entails, as Deleuze would say, affirming the *whole of chance.*

Replika, similarly, responds to a pharmacological moment, but while it appears to be a palliative – an online friend for lonely people (its more monetized sexual agendas aside) – its remedial capacities are largely *adaptive* because it responds to a symptom rather than the problem of broken offline social connections and the concomitant lack of communal rituals and inter- and transgenerational knowledge, or what Stiegler calls *long circuits*. Instead of *inventing* the problem and prefiguring the conditions that allow for the realization of new long circuits – in other words, *adopting* the pharmacological situation by detaching from the *pharmakon* and engaging with other transitional spaces in order to establish new relational consistencies – the app, by and large, engenders an *adaptation* to the pharmacological situation. It is a response to the conditions of the image of thought, to a 'badly stated' question which amounts to a reactively willed nihilism through processes of divestment which, instead of willing *all* of chance, impose 'limitations and partial restrictions on' our affective capacities (*B* 17). Replika is thus a *negation* of all of chance and an affirmation of *reactive* forces that are 'controlled by the spirit of the negative' (*N* 56). Deleuze, drawing on Spinoza, holds that this kind of response does not contain a power identical to Life and, as a result, proliferates and exploits that which causes us to be saddened by the human condition – and this robs us from a feeling that life is worth living (*PP* 12, 25). For Stiegler, this kind of response equals an irrationality, a becoming-unreasonable – which is produced by the short-circuiting of reason itself as we saw in Chapter 4. This gives rise to 'an absence of reasons for living', 'the reversal of all values that is nihilism' (Stiegler 2019: 38). And why would we not will nihilism – absolute negative collective protention – in the face of Anthropogenic doom? Why not give into every base drive? It is certainly more pleasurable than coming to terms with the fact that it may be too late to save the world – at least in some grand-narrative kind of way. Perhaps it is time to consider that The End is what people actually desire – even collectively so.

How do we dream again? What makes life worth living? Is this world still worth fighting for?

These are difficult questions to answer, and certainly more so in the face of ecological collapse. Given this, it makes sense that whole groups of society are opting for VR and gaming – the new 'realer real' – where whole worlds of possibility can be found without ever going anywhere. Why save a doomed planet when you can live online? And anyway, who is to say that living in cyber space is anything different to the illusion that is life? For Deleuze, the answer lies partly in restoring our belief in *this* world because this kind of belief is, for him, intimately linked to the power of fabulation – to the capacity to be affected and affect other bodies in turn. And, as Stiegler says, it is only an affected being that can question, which is to say pose problems. To quote Stiegler:

> Only an affected being can question, which presupposes that it can above all be called into question by its affection. It is in this sense that I refer to uncontrollable societies of disaffected individuals: it is because consumerism has industrially and systemically ruined the process of adoption, that is, of transindividuation, by, as we have described, the systemic imposition of short-circuits, in particular via the conservative revolution, that contemporary pharmacology was held at a purely adaptive stage, ruining the possibility of posing questions on the basis of what, in this pharmacology, called the preceding epochs into question, and in particular modernity.
>
> (Stiegler 2013a: 120)

But to pose problems, or create the right conditions for intensities to circulate so that individuation and transindividuation can occur without being short-circuited, we 'must believe in the body, but as in the germ of life, the seed which splits open the paving-stones, which has been preserved and lives on in the holy shroud or the mummy's bandages, and which bears witness to life, in this world as it is' (*C2* 173). This belief is in that which is incommunicable – the *unthought* and the *untimely* – which is not constrained by the dogmatic image of thought, nor by time in the sense of the present, the eternal or the historical, but is that which acts *counter to* and thus counter-actualizes our time for the benefit of a time yet to come, a people yet to come, but in the here and now (*N* 107). This acting counter to, or counter-actualization, can be thought of in terms of three non-successive moments – moments contained in each other, unfolding through each other or, to put it another way, one moment with three aspects. These three aspects can, moreover, be thought of descriptively as part detective novel, part science fiction novel and part apocalyptic novel. Detective for its posing of problems and concomitant creation of concepts which 'themselves change along with the problems' through practices of what anarchists have described as *prefiguration*, or the creation of metastable conditions that allow for individuation and transindividuation to occur without being short-circuited (*DR* xx). Science fiction for its utopian dimension, the yet-to-come – 'an encounter, as a here-and-now, or rather as an *Erewhon* from which emerges inexhaustibly ever new, differently distributed "heres" and "nows"' (*DR* xx). This is a response to a problem correctly raised 'at the level of practice', a partial and relative resolution of a disparation or tension between two orders – what Stiegler might call *adoption* (*H* 16). And finally, apocalyptic for the throw of the dice, the willing of the eternal return, the secret repetition 'and the secret of an insistence in all our existence', 'a universal ungrounding which turns upon itself and causes only the yet-to-come *to return*' (*DR* 85, 91).

These are some fine lines by Deleuze, as he is fond of saying about other philosophers, but how do we think of these three aspects of counter-actualization practically? This, then, is the aim of this chapter: to theorize the positive project of counter-actualization by bringing together Deleuze, Guattari and anarchism, inflecting and transforming each through the other, making them resonate in continuous variation through a generalized chromaticism: an agitation that wrests consistency from chaos and fabulates new modalities through a combination of the major and the minor.

Life as a detective novel: The posing of problems as prefiguration

In *Chaosmosis*, Guattari asks how we can 'change mentalities' and 'reinvent social practices that would give back to humanity – if it ever had it – a sense of responsibility, not only for its own survival, but equally for the future of all life on the planet' as well as 'incorporeal species such as music, the arts, cinema, the relation with time, love and compassion for others' which engender 'the feeling of fusion at the heart of cosmos?' (*CH* 119–20). Deleuze would tell us that it involves believing in *this* world and posing the right questions, or raising questions to the level of practice because '*the problem always has the solution it deserves*, in terms of the way in which it is stated (i.e., the conditions under which it is determined as problem), and of the means and terms at our disposal for stating it' (*B* 16, emphasis added). Replika, as an answer to the question of loneliness, is deserved in the sense that it responds to a question posed within the conditions set by algorithmic ecologies rather than at the level of the underlying problem, namely what kind of society it is we would like to create and live in.[2] If, however, we understand the algorithm to already present itself as an ethico-political arrangement of values, assumptions and propositions about the world, it changes the problems we pose from *How ought the algorithm be arranged for a good society?* to *What is a good society?* This changes the conditions from which the problem is posed, thereby affecting the order of communication – or the intensive paths – between virtual multiplicities or disparate orders. This is important because problems, according to Deleuze, are of the order of events – they are related to the circulation of intensities in preparation for individuation and transindividuation processes which *contain* the event – because the event is not 'what occurs (an accident)', but what is inside that which occurs, 'the purely expressed' (*LS* 149). The event, moreover, is pharmacological because it presents itself as a wound that we come to embody, that is, it contains the conditions of its treatment. Problems, in other words, are wounding and curative at once, but become increasingly sick or healthy depending on whether we will reactively, which is to say nihilistically, or whether we will the eternal return – the *whole of chance* (*LS* 148). True problems, as we see, thus present themselves as a kind of detective plot which we have to figure out. For anarchists, the method for posing true questions, or figuring out the drama and creating the right conditions for revolutionary breakthroughs – moments of excess or temporary autonomous zones – is *prefiguration.*

Prefiguration is often thought of by anarchists as the deliberate and ethical experimentation that unites means and ends in the here and now (Milstein 2000; Gordon 2017; Raekstad and Gradin 2019: 10). It comprises individual and collective actions *against* domination and *for* the 'development of alternative relationships and ways of being' (Kinna 2016: 202). Even though it involves deliberate experimentation, the aim of prefiguration is *not* 'to establish a foundation for normative judgement' but, rather, to provide 'a general procedure for action that does not rely upon transcendent moral concepts or totalized representations of human nature' (Jun 2012: 131–2). Prefiguration is thus a problem raised at the level of practice and, for anarchists, always involves experimentation. This experimentation, while *informed* by the past – not only 'the anthropological record', but also 'historical events such as the Paris Commune, the Spanish Civil War, the French uprisings of May 1968, the ongoing Zapatista rebellion in Mexico, and the antiglobalization movement', in addition to 'various nonhierarchical, noncoercive social relations, which we already experience in our everyday lives' – is not *constrained* by the past (Jun 2012: 142). In that sense, prefiguration is untimely, yet at the same time intended for the creation of enough consistency – which should be understood here as metastability rather than homeostasis because it promotes disparation, the primer for individuation – to form a base or home, a refrain or ritornello from which a milieu emerges as some protection from the chaos brought about by transitional events or pharmacological situations. This, in turn, creates a productive environment for careful experimentation with, for example, new forms of collectivization, conflict resolution, direct actions, self-management and creativity.

Philosophically, we could say that prefiguration 'sets up' a kind of metastable state between two heterogeneous orders – for instance 'home' or consistency on the one hand, and experimentation 'with the forces of the future, cosmic forces' on the other (*ATP* 311). Between these two different orders there now exists a tension, an asymmetrical 'distribution of potentials' which gives rise to a 'problematic field' where individuation and transindividuation can take place by way of what Simondon calls transduction and Deleuze calls the 'dark precursor' – an order of communication that is both structural and genetic in that it provides the *contingent structure* for the eventual *ontogenetic processes* that give rise to actualization (*DR* 119, 246; see also Simondon 2009: 11). Transduction is thus the intensive path that liberates and actualizes the potential energy in and between pre-individual systems or virtual multiplicities (see Simondon 2017: 156). Prefiguration, accordingly, concerns at least three aspects: consistency (the base or home), experimentation and intensive circuits – where home is as important as experimentation with the new because the one allows for the other to take place without wild destratification and reckless abandonment. Without home, experimentation can become careless and so short-circuit the production of intensive paths. Hence, 'prefiguration contests the frequent and unthinking association of anarchism with destruction, and instead stresses the experimental, productive, and innovative characteristics of anarchist practices that seek to replace or challenge hierarchical and oppressive social forms' (Kinna 2016: 202). Prefiguration is, as such, an experimental and 'shared orientation towards ways of "doing politics" that is manifest across its networks in common forms of organization (anti-authoritarian, non-hierarchical, consensus-based); in a common repertoire of political expression (direct action, constructing alternatives, community outreach, confrontation); in a common discourse and ideology'; and, more generally, 'through "cultural" shared features of dress, music and diet' (Gordon 2007: 33). In short, prefiguration, if undertaken with care, creates the right conditions for the genuinely new to emerge; it produces lines of flight. However, if not undertaken carefully, the lines of flight it creates can become lines of abolition.

Deleuze and Guattari, like anarchists – the latter especially in their theorization of prefiguration – underscore the importance of experimentation for the creation of new ways of thinking and living. In their chapter on the Body without Organs in *A Thousand Plateaus* where they discuss the relationship between consistency, redundancy and experimentation, Deleuze and Guattari present what might be thought of as a kind of manual for immanent, non-prescriptive forms of experimentation. But, although they place emphasis on experimentation, they repeatedly call attention to 'injections of caution' as 'a rule immanent to experimentation' – and here they resonate anarchist understandings of prefigurative experimentation as a fine balance between what is known and what is new (*ATP* 150). The reason they emphasize carefulness is that the Body without Organs,[3] or the plane of consistency – can be botched. Or worse, it can destroy the circuits of desire, unbind the drives and short-circuit individuation and transindividuation processes. 'It is nondesire as well as desire', write Deleuze and Guattari (*ATP* 149). The aim of prefigurative experimentation, if we link it to the BwO, is the careful circulation of intensities – it is a method for learning how to live pharmacologically by *taking care* of the *pharmakon* and, in so doing, not abandoning oneself to reckless deterritorialization. It becomes clear that although there are many ways to produce intensities, not all of these ways are equally beneficial. Deleuze and Guattari give the example of a masochist who creates intensities, and does so well, but these intensities tend to circulate in on themselves, which is not to say that they do not or are incapable of affirming our joyous capacities – they certainly do and can – but they may not be the best kinds of intensities for thinking about how to deal with climate change, for example, even though they may help us prefigure sexual practices that allow for more individual freedom and expression. Moreover, this kind of BwO can trap desire in a circuitous loop so that the conditions for experimentation are always constrained by the need for pain, and pleasure tied to pain. 'For each type of BwO, we must ask: (1) What type is it, how is it fabricated, by what procedures and means (predetermining what will come to pass)? (2) What are its modes, what comes to pass, and with what variants and what surprises, what is unexpected and what expected?' (*ATP* 152). These questions can help us think about our prefigurative practices, the concepts we use to think with and what we are working *towards* rather than achieving.

In a sense, then, prefiguration confronts the question of death – actual death and 'living' death, or the feeling that life is not worth living. Changing the conditions that make life feel worthless is what prefiguration does because it creates habits that help us bind the drives in such a way that a certain amount of consistency can be attained in biopsychical life. Deleuze describes the binding of the drives and the investment of desire as 'a genuine reproductive synthesis, a Habitus', which allows us to passively contract past instances as generalities in the mind so that the future is anticipated on the basis of the past (*DR* 96). We, as subjects, and as collectivities, emerge through these retentional and protentional processes that contract as habits – it is what allows for long circuits to be produced and for adoption to take place, *but* only if we take care to form these habits, to reach a certain level of consistency, to create a refrain to return to in moments of chaos. For Deleuze and Guattari the ritornello is the redundancy that breaches consistency and experimentation – like a tune that is sung by a child in the dark. However, too much redundancy means no experimentation is taking place – life has become stale. Too little redundancy and the organism becomes dismantled. As Deleuze and Guattari remind us, caution is an art:

> You have to keep enough of the organism for it to reform each dawn; and you have to keep small supplies of signifiance and subjectification, if only to turn them against their own systems when the circumstances demand it, when things, persons, even situations, force you to; and you have to keep small rations of subjectivity in sufficient quantity to enable you to respond to the dominant reality. Mimic the strata. You don't reach the BwO, and its plane of consistency, by wildly destratifying.
>
> (*ATP* 160)

From this view, anarchism cannot be 'the Pollyannaish' dream of 'smash the state and everything will be fine' (Seyferth 2009: 281). Rather, it has to provide 'a multi-centered strategy of political diagnosis' – a symptomatology understood as a pharmacological situation, 'a prefigurative strategy of political transformation' that builds networks of 'homes' and practices as habits; and 'a participatory strategy of organizing institutions' that allows for radical but cautious experimentation and which addresses 'the problems and undesirability of the current structures of exclusion and power', while demonstrating 'the desirability and coherency of various alternatives that may take their place' (Nail 2010: 73). It is in this sense that our present is like a detective novel. 'Something happened, something is going to happen, can designate a past so immediate, a future so near, that they are one (as Husserl would say) with retentions and protentions of the present itself' (*ATP* 192–3). Figuring out what happened is how we diagnose the illnesses in society and pose problems at the level of practice which allow us to affirm our affective capacities and denounce 'all that separates us from life' – all the 'transcendent values that are turned against life' (*PP* 26). In short, prefiguration is the primer for the production of long circuits, but it is not enough on its own to construct the revolution – it is only one aspect of counter-actualization.

Life as a science fiction novel: The importance of utopia and the yet-to-come for individuation

If prefiguration is the primer for the production of long circuits, then the utopian dimension of anarchism – the yet-to-come in Deleuzoguattarian thought – is what makes long circuits worth creating. For anarchists, utopia is neither an unattainable ideal or imaginary future place, nor 'a blueprint or rigid plan' (Kinna 2016: 203). Instead, it is thought of in terms of a persistent becoming, 'a stubborn impulse toward freedom and justice – the end of domination, of relations of servitude, and of relations of exploitation', an 'orientation toward what is different, the wish for the advent of a radical alterity here and now' (Abensour 2008: 407). *A memory of the future in the here and now.* Be that as it may, anarchists recognize that utopia is itself a *pharmakon* because it contains, at the same time, the capacity to move us beyond the hopelessness and destruction generated by the State, capitalism and domination more generally, *and* the capacity to function 'as an inert and impotent illusion, a utopia of escape' (Clark 2009: 15). Utopianism can, accordingly, easily become a movement aimed largely, or even solely, against dystopian despair and control without also moving towards more harmonious and participatory ways of living. For anarchists it is important that utopia, while presenting 'positive depictions of polities', should be 'neither static nor perfect' nor essentialist in any way (Seyferth 2009: 284). The aim of utopian thinking is rather to invoke the transformative arrangements that prefiguration aims to establish for the future in the here and now. It is what drives prefiguration or, in more philosophical terms, it is the ground for prefiguration. It is that which allows us to conceive of the yet-to-come, 'to summon forth a new earth, a new people', because it produces the right conditions for *encounters* between politics and its milieu – and encounters are important for the affective traces they leave (*WP* 99).

When we experience an increase in our affective capacities through our invidividual and collective actions, we form powerful memories that inform our habits and help us create a good balance between consistency, redundancy and experimentation. These memories are, properly speaking, retentional syntheses through which protentional circuits are formed that are themselves 'at the origin of new circuits of transindividuation' (Stiegler 2013a: 86). That is, they produce repetitions which, for Deleuze, are the power of difference and differenciation – it is the selection process by which the problems posed become dramatized or actualized in extensity. So, where the detective aspect of counter-actualization is about asking what happened, diagnosing the illnesses in society and posing problems at the level of practice, the science fiction or utopian dimension of counter-actualization constitutes the individuating and transindividuating processes responding to problems, making possible the *adoption* of new pharmacological situations that aid us in reaching a certain amount of consistency or habitus which, when done with care, produces conditions that are conducive for posing questions in such a way that they call forth an encounter with the yet-to-come. This kind of prefigurative, adoptive encounter with the utopian yet-to-come is what produces the event which, although 'impersonal and preindividual in nature', nevertheless requires a 'volitional intuition and a transmutation' from us, that we become the *quasi-cause* 'of what is produced within' and through us and so become worthy of the event (*LS* 148, 149).

> *So how do we become the quasi-cause of what is produced within and through us?*

It involves, first, understanding utopia not as a teleological blueprint, but as the organization of power in a way that is both immanently structural and genetic as we saw in the previous section. If it were a blueprint, the outcomes would be preordained. Understanding utopia as the organization of power or careful circulation of intensities, on the other hand, allows for an understanding of life, 'each living individuality, not as a form, or a development of form, but as a complex relation between differential velocities, between deceleration and acceleration of particles. A composition of speeds and slownesses on a plane of immanence' (*PP* 123). It then becomes a question of understanding the *pharmakon*, or each situation as pharmacological – a question of what is poisonous and what is curative, what 'can decompose other things by giving them a relation that is consistent with one of its own, or, on the contrary, how it risks being decomposed by other things' (*PP* 126). For Deleuze, following Spinoza, these questions are not merely theoretical, they are absolutely concrete. Transposed to radical politics, it means understanding when to speed up action, when to slow down and rest, what kinds of actions and organizations compound our affective capacities for power and joy, and which ones 'decompose' us – emotionally, physically, communally. Understanding these relations of motion and rest and selecting and affirming those forces which expand our individual and collective affective capacities while affirming all of chance – as we will see – is *how* we become the quasi-cause because it enlarges our capacities for affective resonances between individuals and affinity groups that create the right conditions for moments of excess, or the event. Becoming the quasi-cause therefore consists in producing the conditions for the *invention* of a 'way of life that constitutes a new way of taking care of the world, a new way of paying attention to it, through the invention of therapeutics' (Stiegler 2013a: 88). This is especially important for radical politics, where promoting healing and rest is *as* vital as organizing protests or participating in mutual aid programmes like Food Not Bombs. As adrienne maree brown says, we 'all have the capacity to heal each other – healer is a possibility in each of us' (2017: 34). *But* we have to learn to recognize when to rest, when to listen, when to protest, to 'deepen and soften that intelligence such that we can align our behavior, our structures and our movements with our visions of justice and liberation, and give those of us co-creating the future more options for working with each other and embodying the things we fight for – dignity, collective power, love, generative conflict, and community' (brown 2017: 6). This entails, in part, learning to recognize what 'makes desire work in a group, what makes a theory work, an experiment, an art form' and, conversely, what 'makes everything topple into the clutches of a repressive power formation at a given moment' (*LF* 60). Forming systems of care that not only address our individual or collective selves, but also take care of the pharmacological situation itself, is how we build inter- and transgenerational knowledge that leads to healthy habits, propagating a belief in *this* world, all the while opening the present to the future, to the yet-to-come, to utopia.

Another way of thinking about this is in terms of *diagrammatic efficiency* which is all the harder to attain in our contemporary algorithmic ecologies because of the large degree of deference to algorithms in our daily lives. Deleuze and Guattari take their idea of the diagram from Foucault who used it to describe certain regularities that become generalizable. For example, the Panopticon is a generalizable model of the disciplinary organization of power in everyday life. For Deleuze and Guattari, however, the diagram is not only concerned with generalizable regularities, but with thinking the actual or extensive – in other words the world of fully formed subjects and objects – *with* the virtual, which does not here refer to cyberspace, but to the preindividual field of flows and processes which give rise to the world of fully formed objects and subjects. For Deleuze, drawing on Simondon, the virtual or preindividual field provides the 'funds' for the unfolding of being which proceeds through a number of 'phases', of which unity and identity of being are only one; it is only through grasping the full 'dephasing' of being in these processes that we are able to arrive at a full ontogenetic account that does not rely on untenable metaphysical assumptions (Simondon 2009: 6). Hence, if the world is the given, then the virtual or preindividual field is that by which the given is given. It is, in other words, 'genetically prior' to the fully formed world (Simondon 1992: 315). *Thinking* the virtual is important because it is what enables us to think outside of the conditions of the image of thought, to summon the utopian as a new earth and a people yet-to-come. The utopian dimension of counter-actualization is thus the condition from which diagrammatic efficiency emerges, which itself causes intensities to resonate in continuous variation, becoming the quasi-cause of what is produced within and through us.

Life as an apocalyptic novel: Willing the eternal return (the event), or: Making life worth living

The event is not some kind of once-off, overall revolutionary moment that will change the entire world, end capitalism and get rid of all States. Hardly any anarchist thinks that anymore. Moreover, there is no one single event, but multiple events, themselves multiplicities, 'produced in a chaos, a chaotic multiplicity', where chaos, according to a 'cosmological approximation', 'would be the sum of all possibles' (*F* 76, 77). The event, then, is not that which occurs, but that which is *inside* what is occurring – a kind of moment of excess signalling that our 'abstract potential always exceeds and tries to escape the conditions of its production' (The Free Association 2010: 32). To be sure, events are pharmacological: they are the wounds we come to embody. It 'is a question of attaining this will that the event creates in us; of becoming the quasi-cause of what is produced within us' – becoming worthy of the event, 'becoming thereby the actor of one's own events – a *counter-actualization*' (*LS* 148, 150).

It should be clear from the previous two sections that the prefigurative and utopian dimensions of counter-actualization are also pharmacological – prefiguration because it is at once a line of flight and a line of abolition, and utopia because it is concurrently that which calls forth the new earth and the people-to-come and that which keeps us trapped in passive and impotent illusions of escape. Moreover, each of these aspects of counter-actualization is a synthesis of time. Prefiguration, or the posing of problems, is a synthesis of habit as the living present, whereas the utopian aspect is a synthesis of memory as the pure past – a memory of the future which is, properly speaking, the yet-to-come. The synthesis of habit thus presupposes a synthesis of memory: it is the utopian dimension of counter-actualization which makes prefiguration possible. For what are we prefiguring if not a memory of the yet-to-come in the here and now? Similarly, the synthesis of memory presupposes a synthesis of the future or it would not be able to contain the yet-to-come – so the apocalyptic dimension of counter-actualization constitutes a third synthesis of time, a synthesis of the future which allows the self of the past and the present to be brought into a 'secret coherence which excludes that of the self' (*DR* 98). It is thus the third synthesis which allows time itself to unfold, unconditioned by the recursion of personal traumas and fantasies. If the third synthesis is short-circuited, however, it will no longer be *unconditioned* by our past and present, and will simply be a response or adaptation to the conditions of the image of thought rather than that from which the genuinely new emerges. It is for this reason that Deleuze insists that the third synthesis 'refers to the absence of ground into which we are precipitated by the ground itself' (*DR* 114).

As we have seen, the first synthesis, or what we may think of as the first aspect of counter-actualization, has a *binding* function: it binds the drives or Eros 'in the constantly renewed form of a living present' (*DR* 108). Practically speaking this means that the first synthesis facilitates a balance between consistency, redundancy and experimentation. If the drives remained unbound, it would constitute a short-circuiting of primary retention and protention. The first synthesis thus helps us focus on or invest our energies in specific projects, for example prisoner support, free education programmes or DIY workshops. The second synthesis roughly maps to Stiegler's secondary and tertiary retentional and protentional processes. Recall that secondary retentions or functional memory, and tertiary retentions or our externalized hypomnesic memory, contingently and partially condition primary retentions and protentions. Moreover, our collective secondary and tertiary retentions help us form long circuits or inter- and transgenerational memories and practices, so they have an *inscription* and *transference* function. This is why Deleuze links the first synthesis to Eros and the second synthesis to Mnemosyne. The final synthesis, which constitutes the ungrounded form of time or the third aspect of counter-actualization, has a *selection* and *redistributive* function. Deleuze calls this synthesis Thanatos. Like Eros and Mnemosyne, it is pharmacological because it is both that which devitalizes the fluctuations of life and health *and* that which wills the eternal return through the throw of the dice. The throwing of the dice is important because it signals an affirmation of *all of chance* – which includes, but is not limited to, our joyous capacities. Think of the example of Martha who does not affirm or *take care* of her pharmacological situation, namely the death of her partner, Ash. Because she displaces her sadness by increasingly inviting the fake Ash into her life, she fails to embody her wound, willing the situation away reactively. This is not to say that affirming all of chance is 'being okay' with hardship or tyrannical States or capitalism. Certainly not! It means, rather, affirming life despite the presence of death, affirming friendships that make place for sadness and provide comfort, affirming our collective capacities to challenge domination and create alternative ways of living and being, affirming our belief in this world despite the accelerating climate crisis – and doing so in a way that takes care of the *pharmakon*. Put differently, affirming all of chance is an affirmation of contingency. Here, again, we can learn from the Zapatistas who affirm contingency through the practice of *preguntando caminamos*, which roughly translates as 'asking we walk'. This is a radical break with States who are always positing answers and ready-made solutions that determine *in advance* what can unfold. The Zapatistas, by contrast, affirm a more creative and imaginative practice that anticipates and wards off the instalment of the State apparatus in their midst. Far 'from being just another rebellion in some far-off land' they 'challenge us theoretically and practically' to 'conceive differently of politics, of community and of revolution' – of affirmation itself (Holloway 2005). In the words of the Zapatistas: 'Then that suffering that united us made us speak, and we recognised that in our words there was truth, we knew that not only pain and suffering lived in our tongue, we recognised that there is hope still in our hearts' (quoted in Holloway 2011).

This distinction is important because Deleuze and Guattari's concept of affirmation has suffered from both overly optimistic and overly negative interpretations. If we are to use their philosophy for radical politics, we should be clear about what their concepts mean for our practices and thoughts and, more importantly, for how we can create the right conditions for the event and, in so doing, become worthy of the event. To explicate this further, I return here to the actual and virtual or preindividual field. For Simondon, extension – the world of fully formed subjects and objects – does not deplete the preindividual field: 'There is no impoverishment of the information contained in these terms; transduction is characterized by the fact that the result of this operation is a concrete network that contains all the initial terms' (Simondon 2009: 12). But even though actualization does not deplete the preindividual field, the intensive distributions can be contracted or reticulated via short-circuits, as we have seen – so we have to take care of how we produce and affirm these intensive paths. Deleuze, whose concept of the virtual is informed by Simondon's account of the preindividual field, expresses a similar idea: 'We have seen that every process of actualisation was in this sense a double differenciation, qualitative and extensive', he writes, and goes on: 'That is why we proposed the concept of different/ciation to indicate at once the state of differential relations in the Idea or virtual multiplicity *and* the state of the qualitative and extensive series in which these are actualised by being differenciated' (*DR* 245). If the preindividual field or virtual could be depleted, *nothing new could ever emerge again* – that is why actualization or extension constitutes a *relative* solution or chronogenetic and topological phase of the individuation process during which the distribution of intensities is rearranged or *redistributed*. This redistribution is engendered by vice-diction – *differential relations* that determine *how* specific substances will be *expressed*, which is to say unfold or respond to a problematic field (*DR* 48). Vice-diction, then, has 'two procedures which intervene both in the determination of the conditions of the problem and in the correlative genesis of cases of solution: these are, in the first case, the specification of adjunct fields' or multiplicities and, in the second, 'the condensation of singularities' to provoke moments of excess, an abruption which 'causes the Idea to explode into the actual' – the implication being that Ideas and Problems 'do not exist only in our heads but occur here and there in the production of an actual historical world' (*DR* 190). These moments of excess are what contain the event, but becoming worthy of the event necessitates a throw of the dice, or the willing of all of chance, as well as a transmutation or transvaluation of values. If there is no transvaluation, *ressentiment* is willed and affirmed which practically actualizes as anything from microfascism to full-blown tyranny. 'Revolution', writes Deleuze, 'never proceeds by way of the negative' which amounts to little more than the 'objective field of the false problem, the fetish in the person' (*DR* 208). Part of revolutionary struggle is therefore learning how to affirm all of chance – as the Zapatistas teach us – thereby provoking a cut or caesura so that we no longer live in the past and condition the present by past actions, but call forth the yet-to-come, the unconditioned future which now prefigures our actions in the present. In a sense, then, the caesura fractures or wounds the individual – it is the pharmacological moment, the death of the ego, or Thanatos, which can either lead to individual*ization* if ressentiment is affirmed or to individu*ation* and transindividuation which releases the yet-to-come or future dimension of time, and it is precisely the latter which creates a feeling that life is worth living. In a very real sense, then, the third synthesis is about *how* to overcome impotence in life or, put differently, how to affirm life even in the face of death – and this is a question that many anarchists, and also Deleuze and Guattari, have thought of in terms of revolution, which is dealt with in the final chapter.

Tour d'horizon

Living as a being that is capable of being affected and can affect the world in turn has been an important philosophical idea at least since Spinoza. For Deleuze and Guattari this idea is deeply connected to politics and our capacities to collectively produce healthier forms of socio-political organization. In our current algorithmic societies, these capacities have been short-circuited, producing disaffected individuals through the unbinding of the drives and a concomitant withdrawal 'that generates disbelief, miscreance and discredit' – a feeling that life is not worth living (Stiegler 2019: 190). This pervasive condition, which Mark Fisher called *depressive hedonia* and Stiegler terms *abject aboulia*, systemically and systematically destroys our processes of adoption – those processes that help us take care of pharmacological situations – through grammatization and a generalized proletarianization, as we saw in Chapter 4. In other words, the circulation of intensities has become contracted, short-circuiting the individuation and transindividuation processes needed for the formation of long circuits.

In this chapter, we looked at how to create a feeling that life is worth living for the benefit of a time yet-to-come and a people yet-to-come, but in the here and now. I proposed that we think of this in terms of counter-actualization – a process with three aspects that can be thought of descriptively as part detective novel, part science fiction novel and part apocalyptic novel. The first aspect is aimed at figuring out the symptoms of society and posing questions that respond to the real crisis, rather than an image of thought of that crisis. I linked this to the anarchist practice of prefiguration – a practice that binds the drives by creating a congenial space that produces affective connections through, for example, collective organization and the setting up of spaces like infoshops where new habits, such as the practice of nonhierarchical relations, can be fashioned, in turn promoting careful experimentation with different forms of mutual aid or dissent. Prefiguration thus presages the conditions that make life feel worth living by binding and investing the drives in healthier ways; that is, it is the primer for the production of long circuits. The second aspect was allied with the utopian dimension of anarchism and the yet-to-come in Deleuzoguattarian thought. We saw that the aim of utopian thinking is to provide reasons for prefiguration – so prefiguration presupposes the utopian because without some idea of what we are working towards, we will simply give up. The utopian dimension is thus what makes prefiguration worth doing, but the relationship is reciprocal because prefiguration also reinforces the feeling that what we are working towards is worth our time and effort. Finally, we saw that the apocalyptic aspect helps us overcome impotence in life through an affirmation of all of chance, which is to say an affirmation of life even in the face of death, or the apocalyptic. This is important for renewing our belief in *this* world without which we will have few, if any, reasons for living.

In the final chapter, we take a closer look at how counter-actualization is related to revolution, the nomadic war machine, lines of flight and becoming.

Constructing the revolution

Every now and then, in all sorts of different social arenas, we can see moments of obvious collective creation, where our 'excess of life' explodes. In these moments of excess, everything appears to be up for grabs and time and creativity accelerates.

(The Free Association 2010: 32–3)

It had been a cold winter in Petrograd, the strains of the First World War still in the air. The Romanov Empire, now in its 304th year of rule, was clinging desperately to power amid growing tensions on the ground, fuelled by widespread unemployment, hunger and fuel shortages. By February the weather had turned, the uncharacteristic warmth ushering thousands of women into the streets, many congregating on the Nevsky Prospekt to strike for food and suffrage on International Women's Day which, on the old Russian calendar, fell on 23 February 1917. Late that afternoon, on what would become the first day of the February Revolution, men began to join the protests, calling for the abdication of the Tsar amid shouts for bread. A day later, as many as 150,000 workers had joined the demonstrations which would last for another six days, effectively ending the Romanov dynastic rule. With Tsar Nicholas II renounced, the Council of Ministers of Russia was replaced by the Russian Provisional Government. It was not a successful transfer. The government proved to be deeply unpopular, and many turned to the more revolutionary Petrograd Soviet of Workers' and Soldiers' Deputies which was established as a representative body, leading to the situation described as *dvoyevlastiye*, 'dual power'. The committees of the Petrograd Soviet, which were swiftly taken over by the Bolsheviks led by Vladimir Lenin, secured a strong base of support through propaganda that sparked the July Days, a period of instability and armed demonstrations against the Russian Provisional Government. The Government, bent on retaining power, retaliated, killing hundreds of protesters, triggering a temporary decline in Bolshevik popularity.

Lenin, who had meanwhile been in Finland, returned to Russia to call for calm, at which time a warrant for his arrest was issued. To evade arrest, he went into hiding from where he began pushing for a Bolshevik-led insurrection. Although the plan was rejected at first, the Bolshevik Central Committee conceded on 10 October 1917, leading to the October Revolution. Soon after coming into power, the Reds – as the Bolsheviks became widely known – established the Cheka, a secret-police organization aimed at extinguishing any dissent from counterrevolutionaries, especially the 'Whites', a loosely allied confederation of anti-communist forces. Mass executions were carried out in Penza and Nizhniy Novgorod to put an end to various protests which saw over 10,000 people killed in the first two months. The gulag system was also implemented, doubling the average daily prison population between 1900 and 1914 (CrimethInc. 2019). The Reds, in the interim, focused their energies on expansion, invading the Ukraine on 7 January 1919 with an army led by Vladimir Antonov-Ovseyenko, Joseph Stalin and Volodymyr Zatonsky, helped along and fought against by the anarchists through a culmination of two forces of nature – Maria Nikiforova and Nestor Makhno.

Nikiforova, who was born in the Ukrainian town of Aleksandrovsk in 1885, was 'the daughter of an officer who had been a hero of the last Russo-Turkish War' (Archibald 2007). At a relatively young age, Maria found work as a bottle washer in a vodka distillery and 'joined a local group of anarcho-communists', becoming a fully fledged *boevik* or militant almost overnight. The group advocated for *bezmotivny* or motiveless terror to destabilize agents of economic repression, especially the monarch 'who was an honorary member of the "Union of the Russian People", an organization roughly equivalent to the Klu Klux Klan' (Archibald 2007). At the time, it was not only anarchists who resorted to terror. 'All the socialist groups used terror. In fact, even middle-class liberals endorsed the use of terror against tsarist repression' (Archibald 2007). Against this backdrop, Nikiforova took part in a bomb attack on a passenger train and, although no one was seriously injured, the wealthier passengers were horrified. By 1908, after a few more such incidents, the police closed in, leading to an attempted suicide by Maria but, when the bomb failed to explode, she was arrested and imprisoned. The court at first sentenced her to death but because she was younger than twenty-one – the recognized age of adulthood in the Russian Empire – the sentence was commuted to twenty years' hard labour.

Marusya, as she had become known, did not spend long in Siberia, escaping via the taiga to the Great Siberian Railway, from which she reached Vladivostok, and then Japan. Aided by student-anarchists who bought her a ticket to the United States, she found temporary shelter amongst anarchist-emigrants in New York and Chicago. Around 1912, Marusya returned to Europe where she remained active in various capacities until the revolution broke out in Russia in 1917 when she made her way back to her hometown. Upon her arrival, Nikiforova found that a local Anarchist Federation, consisting of about 300 members, 'had been set up, though they had little influence on local events at the time' (Archibald 2007). Marusya soon changed this, learning of another anarchist group, the Anarcho-Communist Group led by Nestor Makhno, also the commander of the Revolutionary Insurrectionary Army of Ukraine, generally referred to as the *Makhnovshchina* or the Makhnovists – a social movement made up largely of peasant guerrilla groups in the region. The two teamed up, mobilizing the Black Guard – a peasant army consisting of hundreds of men, predominantly anarchists who entered into several formal military alliances with the Red Army to defeat the White Army – even though Makhno considered the Bolsheviks a threat to the development of the anarchist Free Territory within the Ukraine. His suspicions would be confirmed when the Red Army eventually betrayed the anarchists. For the time being, though, they enjoyed the ear of one of the commanders of the Soviet forces in Ukraine, Antonov-Ovseyenko, who was very taken by Marusya – so much so that he appointed her as 'commander of a formation of cavalry detachments in steppe Ukraine' and 'allocated a significant sum of money to her' which she used to kit out a fleet of trains compared to the Flying Dutchman for its likelihood 'to appear at any time, anywhere' (Archibald 2007).

They appeared on lines of fight, as packs, as deterritorialized intensities at the intersection of milieus, lodged on a stratum, finding advantageous places on it, tapping into latent movements and potential experiments, constructing a plane or diagram, drawing the wandering lines of drift that gave way to lines of flight. There is nothing symbolic or imaginary about the black train, commandeered by the Free Combat Druzhina, armed to the teeth yet adorned with banners. Long Live Anarchy! The Liberation of the Workers is the Affair of the Workers Themselves! Power Breeds Parasites! Anarchy is the Mother of Order! Small wonder Deleuze thinks real revolutions 'have the atmosphere of fetes' (DR 268).

Roughly a year later, on 9 February 1918, a peace treaty was signed between the Ukrainian Central Rada and the Central Powers, a peace that was not felt in Elizavetgrad. 'With German forces approaching the city the Bolsheviks hurriedly began to evacuate their troops and institutions, leaving a power vacuum' (Archibald 2007). The Druzhina returned to the city which was at first marked by 'several days of peace between the new civic authorities and the anarchists', the latter of whom 'took over the railway station and annoyed the citizens mainly by singing anarchist songs' (Archibald 2007). The short-lived peace was broken when a robbery at the huge Elvorta plant was credited to the anarchists, even though it was regarded by Marusya as an incitement by right-wing elements. The Bolsheviks decided to neutralize the Druzhina but, by the time they had finally issued a call for an arrest, the anarchists had slipped away. 'Heading east, the Druzhina stopped at the station of Tsarekonstantinovka where Marusya ran into a disconsolate Nestor Makhno. A nationalist military coup in Gulyai-Pole had just resulted in the arrest of the local Revkom and Soviet while Makhno was absent' (Archibald 2007). The pair tried to coordinate a rescue mission but received word that the Germans had occupied the line they would need to get to Gulyai-Pole. Marusya was arrested anon, though she was soon released again after being acquitted of all charges. Both finding themselves in Taganrog, Marusya and Makhno teamed up one last time, this time to present 'a series of lectures in the local theatre and various workplaces', but they soon split up again (Archibald 2007). Makhno, exiled in August 1921, made his way to Berlin where he would meet members of the Free Workers' Union of Germany (FAUD), including Rudolph Rocker, finally ending up in Paris, where he spent the rest of his life working as a carpenter and stagehand at the Paris Opera and various film studios. He died in Paris on 25 July 1934 from tuberculosis. Marusya was not as lucky. Recognized on a street in Sevastopol on 11 August 1919, she and her husband were both arrested. At her trial before General Subbotin, roughly two months later on 16 September 1919, she was accused of shooting 'officers and peaceful inhabitants', as well as 'bloody, merciless' insurrections for which she was found guilty and sentenced to death (Archibald 2007). She was shot to death, but the legend of the revolutionary black train lives on, a line of flight without beginning or end.

A nomadic war machine, like the war machine described by Clastres, invented by the nomads to ward off the State apparatus. It is a strange machine, this war machine whose primary object is not war, even though it is always warring, inventing new weapons on lines of flight. 'A revolutionary machine, all the more abstract for being real' (ATP 512).

The nomadic war machine

In Chapter 2, we looked at two of the three interrelated concepts developed by Deleuze and Guattari in their work on the State apparatus, namely the *Urstaat* and *capture*. Recall that the theory of the *Urstaat* was developed to challenge evolutionism, or the idea that the State is a natural product of the progression of society from savagery to barbarism to civilization. Drawing on Clastres, Deleuze and Guattari argue, instead, that the State 'comes into the world fully formed and rises up in a single stroke' (ATP 427). What they mean by this is that statism and nonstatism are immanent to each other because they each form the limit-point for the other after which a threshold is crossed. Think about it this way: The *Urstaat* is an abstraction of the latent, but *real*, possibility of the State at the limit of statelessness, just as the *nomadic war machine*, the third concept developed alongside the *Urstaat* and the *apparatus of capture*, is the abstraction of the latent, and thus real, possibility of life against and outside of the State. Because it is an *abstract machine* or *diagram*, which is to say an unformed or not yet actualized intensity, the nomadic war machine can assume many different forms in extensity, though it is marked by its operations *against* the State, whether via 'insubordination, rioting, guerrilla warfare, or revolution as act' (ATP 386). Marusya's black train, accordingly, is an actualized instantiation of the nomadic war machine.

In the twelfth chapter of *A Thousand Plateaus*, titled '1227: Treatise on Nomadology – The War Machine', Deleuze and Guattari distinguish the nomadic war machine from State military institutions in terms of three aspects – a spatiogeographic aspect, an arithmetic or algebraic aspect and an affective aspect. The first aspect is related to the composition of territory, or the logics according to which the nomadic war machine proceeds territorially. These differ markedly from those of the State apparatus which proceeds via a territorial logic that is profoundly deterritorializing *and* reterritorializing, as we saw in the first two chapters. The State, in other words, deterritorializes existing codes to overcode them via stratifications, including those of race and gender, just as it deterritorializes the earth to overcode or reterritorialize it on striating grids for the purposes of rent and taxation. The nomadic war machine, on the other hand, is distributive rather than striating. Instead of gridding space, 'assigning each person a share and regulating the communication' between the grids, the nomadic war machine 'distributes people (or animals) in an open space, one that is indefinite and noncommunicating' (*ATP* 380). Although this distribution is also a deterritorialization, it is not aimed at sedentary reterritorialization, as is the case with the State apparatus, but constitutes a rhythmic method that promotes minor movements over molar modes of socio-political organization. However, as Deleuze and Guattari warn, this deterritorialization, which is a smoothing of space, is not enough 'to save us' – 'smooth spaces are not in themselves liberatory' because 'smooth space and the form of exteriority do not have an irresistible revolutionary calling but change meaning drastically depending on the interactions they are part of and the concrete conditions of their exercise or establishment' (*ATP* 500, 387). In plain words, context is important. A nomadic war machine can just as easily lead to more liberatory practices as be appropriated by the State apparatus because these two limit points are immanent to each other. Nevertheless, the territorial *tendency* of the nomadic war machine is towards decentralization whereas the territorial tendency for the State apparatus is towards stratification. Take, for example, State military institutions which are generally characterized by rigid hierarchical relations, a clear-cut chain of command, a certain uniformity and conformity, a common language and a strict need-to-know principle for the sharing of information. Contrast this to some of the practices of the Zapatistas we have looked at that can be thought of in terms of the nomadic war machine, like *mandar obedeciendo*, or 'leading by obeying', according to which leaders govern by submitting their authority to the collective decisions of their communities, or *preguntando caminamos*, translated as 'asking we walk', an emergent strategy or cartographic method that confirms contingency and immanence rather than transcendent frameworks.

The second aspect is arithmetic or algebraic. Deleuze and Guattari again give the example of State military organizations, arguing that they *resemble* nomadic numerical organization in some ways: clans and lineages are resembled by, for example, 'units, companies, and divisions' (*ATP* 387). The reason for this semblance, Deleuze and Guattari suggest, is that the principle of numerical organization is adopted from nomadic peoples. This is because the State apparatus 'has no war machine of its own; it can only appropriate one in the form of a military institution' (*ATP* 355). So, when the State creates armies, it adopts the principle of numerical organization 'at the same time as it appropriates the war machine' (*ATP* 387). What changes, though, is the method of inscription, which is no longer directly invested in the earth, as we saw in Chapter 1, but now functions according to a new logic, namely overcoding, which effectuates a change in the relationship to number. In other words, whereas arithmetic organization is relatively autonomous in nomadic societies where peoples are distributed in space, this changes when the war machine is appropriated by the State apparatus which distributes or striates space itself. The earth now becomes divided into plots that can be counted just as people are counted for the purposes of tax, elections and census. This 'arithmetic element' of the State is expressed through imperial bureaucracy and its attendant calculation techniques, a 'whole social calculus' through which the State finds its 'specific power' that primarily striates matters and secondarily stratifies people according to numbers – demography and other statistical measurements being paradigmatic – which serves always to 'gain mastery over matter' and control all 'variations and movements' according to a specific 'spatiotemporal framework' (*ATP* 389). Instead of differentiation, specialization and the concentration of power in a central body, the revolutionary war machine mobilizes number in complex ways that amount to a doubling along two nonsymmetrical series so that its power is not located in segments and centres that resonate with each other according to an overcoded logic, but in a dynamic formation that implies a deterritorialization *and* a becoming (*ATP* 391–3). The nomadic war machine, in other words, is an *emergent strategy*, a black train on a line of flight, a becoming, an interval or intermezzo, a 'texture' that 'can be crafted in such a way as to lose fixed and homogeneous values, becoming a support for slips in tempo' that mobilizes a passional regime of affects, so facilitating the binding of the drives for the creation of what Stiegler calls long circuits (*ATP* 478). Deleuze and Guattari explain: 'Assemblages are passional, they are compositions of desire' which 'has nothing to do with a natural or spontaneous determination; there is no desire but assembling, assembled, desire' (*ATP* 399).

This, then, is the third aspect of the nomadic war machine: that it assembles and mobilizes affects – not feelings – as a weapon, as an emergent power that is central to the Spinozian-Deleuzian lineage. These emergent powers 'are not about controlling things but about *response-ability*, capacities to remain responsive to changing situations. This is why they are a bit paradoxical: they are *material* ideas, accessed by tuning into the forces that compose us, inseparable from the feelings and practices that animate them' (Montgomery and bergman 2017: 32). When people, individually and collectively, affirm their capacities to 'participate in something life-giving', they 'often become more militant' – a nomadic war machine – which may at times be expressed as 'the struggle against internalized shame and oppression', and at other times as a 'fierce support for a friend or loved one; the courage to sit with trauma; a quiet act of sabotage; the persistence to recover subjugated traditions; drawing lines in the sand; or simply the willingness to risk' (Montgomery and bergman 2017: 30). The nomadic war machine, in other words, expresses a joyful militancy, a 'politics that is constructive and prefigurative', which is not to 'deny that political engagement often involves suffering' – of course it does – but 'the joy is knowing and deciding that we can do something about it; it is recognizing that we share our pain with other people', and it is 'feeling the solidarity of those around us' (Federici quoted in Montgomery and bergman 2017: 244). It is fighting the Red Army on this side, the White Army on that, *and* singing anarchist songs in celebration. *A joyful militancy according to which affect is mobilized as a weapon.* A process which involves learning 'to undo things, and to undo oneself', by which Deleuze and Guattari do not mean wild destratification, but an undoing of the State apparatus in oneself (*ATP* 400). This undoing is a double movement: the undoing of the State apparatus and the becoming capable of acting, of doing something new – and it is precisely this becoming capable of acting that is revolutionary, as we will see.

Viva la révolution!

Revolution, like any other concept from the anarchist milieu, can only be understood as part of a constellation of concepts, though it has, since the inception of anarchism, been resolutely against reform through vanguardist programmes. This rejection of reform is grounded in an understanding that content necessarily follows form and vice versa. If the form remains statist, it will necessarily be filled with statist content, as the Russian Revolution has clearly shown.[1] Thus, if we want to live in societies that are closer to the anarchist ideals we have, our revolutionary practices need to prefigure what we are aiming for, because the problems we pose always get the solutions they deserve, as we saw in Chapter 5. Vanguardist programmes, moreover, involve a level of representation which anarchists think is largely unnecessary, first of all because it separates us from our capacity to act and participate directly in the conditions of our lives and, second, because it severs us from our capacities to be affected by the world and affect the world in turn because this capacity is always arbitrated. Affects thus intermediated are mobilized as weapons against us. Stated differently, political representation mediates affects because it provides certain images to people 'of who they are and what they desire', thereby arresting their 'ability to decide those matters for themselves' (May 1994: 48). Anti-representation, on the other hand, is an ethical principle freed from transcendent frameworks and intermediaries. As such, it creates 'the conditions in which we can respond to reality' – rather than an image of reality – and so 'increase our capacity to be "ethical" by demanding recognition of all the relations involved' in any given event (Vasileva 2019: 115). It is for these reasons that anarchists view revolution as that which 'seeks to alter the whole character of society' (Berkman 1972: 293) with 'the hope of seeing something arise to improve' future conditions (Kropotkin 1892) even though it is not per se 'a thing of the future but the present, not a matter of demands, but of living' (Landauer 1978: 107). In addition to prefiguration and anti-representation as key revolutionary practices, Proudhon and Kropotkin understand the revolution symptomatologically, which is to say as an interrogation of historical conditions. For Kropotkin, revolution is deeply concerned with the construction of utopia which it achieves, at least in part, by diagnosing the illnesses of the current situation and learning from this how to 'organize the accumulation of wealth and its reproduction in the interest of the whole of society' (Kropotkin 1892). Following from this, Proudhon views the revolution as that which renews the world and, 'in renewing it', also conserves it (Proudhon 1848). A symptomatology is thus one of the primary measures implemented in revolutionary practices because it provides the means for diagnosing the symptoms of society, formulating or posing problems at the level of practice, and fabulating more therapeutic ways of living to renew and conserve the world. But revolution is not a single occurrence or even several incidents; it is, rather, 'one permanent revolution' (Proudhon 1848).

Here we find two important overlaps with the philosophy of Deleuze and Guattari: first in terms of symptomatology and, second, in terms of the idea that revolution is a continuous movement, a ceaseless becoming-revolutionary or 'dynamic efficiency' – 'a constructivism, a "diagrammatism", operating by the determination of the conditions of the problem and by transversal links between problems' (*ATP* 559, 473). This constructivism does not refer to 'what is traditionally understood as "social constructivism" in sociology and philosophy, namely, that revolutions are by-products or "social constructs" produced by human minds, language, institutions, historical contexts, cultural values and so on' (Nail 2012: 21). It is, rather, constructivist in the sense that it assembles or fabricates – one might even say *fabulates* – revolutionary connections operating transversally across molar lines, molecular lines and lines of flight, maximizing 'relations of molecular potential', but always 'in the living mode, as a function of collective assemblages with changing contours' and 'praxes that rebel against sociological and economic invariants' (*LF* 52; see also *D* 96). Revolution is thus that which conjuncts politics with the present milieu. It is marked both by periods of 'very slow changes' – what is sometimes referred to as the *social revolution* – and periods of 'violent changes', both of which are necessary (Kropotkin 1892). The slower periods – or what Deleuze and Guattari refer to as plateaus – are especially important for the construction of long circuits which, when pierced by moments of climax, excess or *haecceity*, provide the necessary consistency or continuity needed for integrating the inevitable redistribution of the sensible associated with more climactic events or moments, as we saw in Chapter 5 (*ATP* 507).

For many anarchists, revolution comprises both destructive and constructive dimensions. On the one hand, revolution is aimed at the abolishment of capitalism, private property and wages, together with the destruction of the State and its repressive forces, including the police, prisons, the military and the judiciary (Kropotkin 1892; Malatesta 1922). But, as Deleuze tells us, good 'destruction requires love'; it is easy to criticize 'vulgarity' and 'complacency' but recognizing that we also love some of what we want to destroy is more courageous (*DI* 139). It is the difference between simply escaping and constructing a line of flight, the latter of which takes place while looking for a weapon. This weapon is not just any weapon, however, but the *nomadic war machine* whose object is 'not war, but the drawing of a creative line of flight' (*ATP* 422), which constitutes the more constructivist aspect of revolution and is aimed at replacing the State by federated groups of individuals working together and experimenting with more liberatory 'forms of society' in order to provoke a 'social transformation in all its broad complexity' (Malatesta 1922). Deleuze echoes Malatesta here for whom the problem of building new social relations with new kinds of intensities and activities in a common space without private property is the real problem of revolution (*DI* 145). So the constructivist component is really more important than the destructive aspect, even though revolution is often thought of more in terms of violent demolition, because if we do not have new institutions, relations and practices to replace capitalist and State organizations and their associated habitudes – which includes very practical aspects like food distribution, waste management and different kinds of family structures – we will almost inevitably fall back on older creations, oftentimes simply because they are there. This is why revolution, for Malatesta, is concerned with the creation of new living conditions vis-à-vis more just institutions, the free and equal groupings of individuals for the production of healthier social relationships, the creation of sustainable ethical and material conditions, the organization of public services by all for all and the coordination of the desires and interests of all people in such a way that it promotes the freedom of all (1995: 41–2). As Luigi Fabbri says: 'The function of anarchism is not so much to prophesy a future of freedom, but to prepare it' (1921).

This preparation has, at times, included violent action – and it is precisely the question of violence in revolutionary action that is often used to charge anarchists and anarchism with unnecessary aggression and brutality, especially given the history of 'propaganda by the deed' which developed in the late nineteenth century, though it was, as we saw from Marusya's history, a practice endorsed widely outside of anarchist circles as well. Natasha Lennard's concept of *counterviolence* is useful here, which she uses to think about the use of violence not so much in terms of necessary secondary violence, but in terms of '*impossible nonviolence*' (2019: 22). Counterviolence is thus violence against the originary violence of State and capitalism when no other possibility for movement exists. War or violence is, after all, not the primary objective of the nomadic war machine. These conditions come about when society no longer provides the necessary means for constructing consistency between thoughts, 'words, gestures and life', in large part due to the perpetual modulation infused into society by the State, capitalism, algorithmic ecologies and their attendant structures (The Invisible Committee 2009: 17). This constant modulation, which is aimed at rendering political agents little more than consumers, expresses an instantaneous incorporeal transformation which not only transforms people into subjugated and addicted consumers at a stroke, but also deprives them of their collective or assemblaged capacities for enunciation, which is to say their capacities to construct political consistency outside the order-words or 'semiotic coordinates' of the State and capitalism (*ATP* 75).

Order-words, Deleuze and Guattari tell us, are the 'elementary unit of language', that element which conveys information, though this conveyance is not for knowledge transfer, but for compelling obedience (*ATP* 76). Order-words, in other words, communicate a condition of possibility – a 'silent order' of things as Foucault would say (*ATP* 87). The question is not so much about how to 'elude the order-words' as it is about how to escape the 'death sentence it envelopes' and how to do so without falling into a black hole (*ATP* 110). In practical terms it involves thinking about how to live as much outside of capitalism without falling into the traps of other kinds of individualism, for example 'trustafarianism' or guru-seeking behaviours. This involves understanding how order-words are transmitted, for example how the education of a person is always assimilated to their training as a worker, itself assimilated to the 'apprenticeship of the soldier', all of which are assimilated to the domestication of the consumer (*ATP* 399). In place of a consistency between thoughts, words, gestures and life, the world is overcoded with order-words or 'canons of behaviour' formed 'from fairly precise rules' which 'capital has learned to control perfectly', providing the impression that there is room for participation in 'public affairs' (Bonanno 2009: 17). Such processes of exclusion deprive people of a common language – which is not the same as 'tongue' – for producing shared practices like solidarity and communism, based on a 'common recognition of the concept of equality' (Bonanno 2009: 26). This reduced capacity for communal languages, gestures and practices functions, on the one hand, to exclude people from the included power structures of dominant forces and, on the other hand, to pacify them, essentially 'keeping the exploited quiet' (Bonanno 2009: 40). Revolutionary violence is not only a response to State and capitalist violence, but an affirmation according to which people once again come to recognize themselves as more than consumers, thereby beginning to construct a revolutionary passage to produce conditions that make life worth living.

This means that all methods have their place, that all the fronts of struggle are necessary, and that all levels of participation are important. This is about an inclusive process, which is anti-vanguard and collective. The problem with the revolution (pay attention to the small letters) is then no longer a problem of THE organization, THE method, THE *caudillo*. It becomes rather a problem which concerns all those who see that revolution is necessary and possible, and whose achievement is important for everyone.

(Marcos 2004: 164)

This involves, at the very least, an understanding of revolutionary conditions, revolutionary concrete practices and the revolutionary political subject.

Revolutionary conditions, concrete practices and subject groups

In *Returning to Revolution*, a book that brings together the philosophy of Deleuze and Guattari with the revolutionary theory, practices and struggles of the Zapatistas – short for the Zapatista Army of National Liberation (*Ejército Zapatista de Liberación Nacional*, EZLN), a largely indigenous political group in Chiapas, Mexico's southernmost state – Thomas Nail thinks about some of the elements needed to create a consistent, participatory and revolutionary body politic. He argues that the Zapatistas invent a new body politic whose revolutionary abstract machines, or 'conditions for social order and inclusion' are consistent with 'the concrete elements and subjects' thereof (Nail 2012: 138). For him, *Zapatismo*, as a kind of permanent revolution, provides the right conditions for a new social order to emerge *and be sustained*. That is, it works according to a set of logics that is 'of the order of the event, of becoming or of the haecceity' because it forms a kind of relay between the virtual – the plane of consistency, matter or the Planomenon – and the actual or extensive, what Deleuze and Guattari also refer to as *formed matters* or the Ecumenon (*ATP* 264, 73). As a relay between the virtual and the extensive, the abstract machine emits and combines particles from these two different planes to achieve diagrammatic efficiency, thus creating the right conditions for revolutionary practices and subjectivities to be developed and achieve a certain amount of consistency (*ATP* 56). The virtual and actual thus presuppose individuation so that a change in one effectuates a change in the other because it redistributes the field of intensities, which is to say that diagrammatic efficiency for revolutionary conditions can only be achieved if there is some consistency between the conditions from which revolutionary concrete practices and subjects emerge. If revolutionary subjects begin to turn to more statist practices, new thresholds of consistency will emerge which could see a more reactionary type of desire existing alongside the revolutionary investment, even replacing it at some point in time (*AO* 105).

Once the right conditions for revolution have been achieved for a new body politic to emerge, these have to be sustained through concrete practices 'that effectuate and react back on their conditions' (Nail 2012: 140). One of the practices Nail identifies is the thirty-eight autonomous municipalities into which roughly 2,200 Zapatista communities are federated. The municipalities are further grouped into five *Juntas de Buen Gobierno* (JBG) or Councils of Good Government 'committed to, among other things, autonomy, participatory self-government, consensus decision-making, respect for nature and life without the use of pesticides', as well as non-discriminatory practices in terms of gender, religion, race and so on (Nail 2012: 106; see also Marcos 2006). These practices reflect an investment of desire and interest consistent with the revolutionary goals of Zapatismo – a becoming-revolutionary constructed from the understanding that the revolution is not spontaneist even if it is an immanent experiment on a molecular line constructed by people themselves (*D* 96, 145). It is for this reason that Deleuze and Guattari say that desire is part of the infrastructure – because it really produces the reality we construct and invest in and so becomes part and parcel of the foundation of society. This is not to say that such concrete practices are 'normative', 'goal-driven' or revisionist; rather, they are consistent and revolutionary 'in the sense that instead of applying solutions to pre-given problems (how to make sure everyone is represented fairly in a presupposed state, for example), or simply affirming that "other problems are possible", particular problems are themselves transformed directly by those who effectuate them and who are affected by them' (Nail 2012: 126). This is what Deleuze means by 'becoming capable' of acting and so worthy of the event (*DR* 90). It is one thing knowing what needs to be done; becoming capable of doing so, however, marks the caesura or point of no return – the point after which the action taken will cause life to never be the same again. These revolutionary concrete practices do just that: they change actualized life by changing the conditions from which living practices emerge. They also change the subjects who emerge from these conditions and practices.

Becoming capable of acting is, for Deleuze and Guattari, linked to what they call the two positive tasks of schizoanalysis. The first task is pharmacological because it is aimed at undoing all the reterritorializations that transform the poisonous or sick elements of society into institutionalized madness (*AO* 321). A good example of this is how depression or ADHD becomes diagnosed as the affairs of individuals rather than as symptoms of a sick society created by the State, capitalism and algorithmic ecologies. This is not to say that there are not real neurobiological reasons for depression or ADHD; it is, rather, drawing attention to the fact that the proliferation of these illnesses in our societies has structural correlates as well. Another example is how liberatory identity struggles become subsumed under neoliberal guises which strip them of their initial revolutionary desire and trap them in consumerist investments. This is why Stiegler emphasizes the importance of *taking care* of *pharmaka* – because they are at once 'the condition of possibility (of consistence) as well as of impossibility (of inexistence)' (Stiegler 2013a: 78). Deleuze and Guattari, in a similar vein, underscore the importance of diagnosing 'the nature, the formation' and the 'functioning' of assemblages or desiring-machines, because not doing so can transform the freed lines of intense becomings into more destructive 'deliriums and hallucinations' (*AO* 322, 330). It is not enough to liberate flows of desire – they have to be reinvested and continually assessed for new microfascisms. This, then, is the second positive task of schizoanalysis: 'to reach the investments of unconscious desire of the social field, insofar as they are differentiated from the preconscious investment of interest, and insofar as they are not merely capable of counteracting them, but also of coexisting with them in opposite modes' (*AO* 350). Differently stated, our desires and interests have to align so that there is consistency between our thoughts, words and actions. This entails understanding not only the molar oppressions and aggregates of society – such as those induced by the State, capitalism, patriarchy, racism and so on – but also the 'molecular multiplicities of singularities' that circulate in and between assemblages. These molecular intensities can be healthy or poisonous – they are *pharmaka* which can unbind the drives through adaptation processes or invest the drives via adoption processes (*AO* 366).

Inventing new forms of subjectivity, it should be clear by now, is as important as changing practices and prefiguring revolutionary conditions. For the Zapatistas, this new form of subjectivity is the *compa* who, instead of revelling in the glory and accomplishments of the individual, accentuates the power of collectivity which they do practically by wearing masks. The 'collective practice of masking has produced a very specific kind of revolutionary subjectivity immanent not to a consciousness who represents an "I" to itself, but to the event: to Zapatismo itself' (Nail 2012: 145). This kind of subjectivity opposes vanguardism in that it deindividualizes people by creating a kind of generic Zapatismo subjectivity that is expressed collectively through what might be thought of as an *imperceptible subject-group*. Deleuze and Guattari distinguish between subject-groups and subjugated groups, taking care to note that all groups are always mixtures of the two, though each of these exhibits certain tendencies that characterize them. A subjugated group, accordingly, is marked by its predisposition to mechanisms of control and repression; that is, having its own desires subsumed by something or someone outside of it, for example capitalism, the State, other identity groups and so on (*AO* 348; *PT* 76). The subject-group, on the other hand, organizes itself transversally, expresses its own interests and produces tools for achieving what it desires, but does so with the understanding that life is not a series of causal links according to which life can be planned and played out absolutely – in other words, without recourse to transcendent forms (*AO* 348, 377; *PT* 107). Having said this, it is important to understand that even though a subject-group expresses more collective agency, there is no valence attached to it – a subject-group can be fascist just as easily as it can be anarchist. What makes the Zapatista model positive is that it rejects neoliberal as well as individualized subjectivity in favour of a collective subjectivity that is of the order 'of the event itself' (Nail 2012: 145). This is partly achieved through the becoming-imperceptible – which is not the same as becoming invisible – of subject-group members. To become imperceptible, according to Deleuze and Guattari, is to dismantle 'love in order to become capable of loving. To have dismantled one's self in order finally to be alone and meet the true double at the other end of the line' – in other words, it is to dismantle oneself from the facializations that bind us to structures of domination (*ATP* 197).

The masked *compa* is, first of all, a becoming-minoritarian, a political affair that is an active micropolitics aimed at disrupting faciality (*ATP* 292). Recall that faciality is a function of majoritarian redundancy in that it sets up groups of domination that become the standard against which all other groups are measured, 'white man' being both paradigmatic and the redundancy. Becoming-minoritarian should not be confused with a minority identity, such as racial or gendered groups within a State (*ATP* 291). It is true that Zapatistas are a minority in that sense but, more importantly, is that the *compa* is a becoming-minoritarian in the sense that it is an asignifying rupture – rather than a 'signifying break' as a minority would be – because it ruptures faciality: it is 'a line of flight forever in the process of being drawn' (*ATP* 24, 207). It is a double movement which consists in the *withdrawal* of the minority from the majority and the *coming into* of the minority (*ATP* 291). The practice of collective masking in Zapatismo thus wards off vanguardism 'insofar as it creates a visual equality between subjects without leaders' and representation insofar as it 'de-individualises first person subjects in favour of third person collective subjects of the event' (Nail 2012: 154). In a continual movement of becoming, the *compa* moves through a becoming-minoritarian to a becoming-revolutionary – a becoming process that 'remains indifferent to questions of a future and past of the revolution' because it moves *between* the two as an untimely haecceity along a transversal line towards another becoming, a becoming-imperceptible, 'the immanent end of becoming, its cosmic formula' (*ATP* 292, 279). The *compa* thus prefigures a revolutionary subjectivity as a bloc, *like the black blocs*, like a building block, part of a larger block, at times a shield, at other times a weapon, a bloc of affects, a bloc of expression, a mode of expansion, 'propagation, occupation, contagion, peopling' (*ATP* 239). *They are legion, we are legion, I am legion.*

Tour d'horizon

'History', write Deleuze and Guattari, 'is made by those who oppose history (not by those who insert themselves into it, or even reshape it)' (*ATP* 295). It is *another history*, a minor history, one that takes place on the streets, under the pavement, in the black train, always on a line of flight, always on the lookout for an encounter, for a weapon: the making of a nomadic war machine. It is the history of revolutions, even those considered failures, especially those considered failures. Failure, after all, is an immanent criterion of experimentation. Take May 1968 which, from a macropolitical point of view, was understood as a failure, which is to say that it was not understood at all, for 'something unaccountable was escaping' (*ATP* 216), a molecular flow 'breaking with causality', a 'bifurcation, a deviation with respect to laws, an unstoppable condition' opening up 'a new field of the possible' (*TR* 233). The event is always that which takes place *inside* what is occurring. *But* we have to become the quasi-cause for the event to occur. We have to create the right conditions through a becoming-revolution, a continual process that constructs or invents a new body politic whose revolutionary abstract machines are consistent with the concrete elements and subjects thereof so that moments of excess can be sustained as plateaus of intensity. Deleuze and Guattari call plateaus 'any multiplicity connected to other multiplicities' (*ATP* 22) that 'form or extend a rhizome' – a new model of thinking and organizing defined by 'an endless, haphazard multiplicity of connections, which is not dominated by a single centre or place, but rather is decentralised and plural' (Newman 2003). To be sure, revolutionary becoming is a process aimed at changing *everything* – from the way in which we conceive of power to the kinds of relationships we build to the shared practices of meaning we create. Anarchy, then, is 'what happens wherever order is not imposed by force' but unfolds, rather, as process of freedom, 'the process of continually reinventing ourselves and our relationships' (CrimethInc. n.d.). It is an emergent strategy that 'emphasizes critical connections over critical mass' (brown 2017: 3). It is an emerging subjectivity, one that is continually passing from one becoming to the next, distributing intensities that give rise to a problematic field where processes of individuation and transindividuation can take place. A joyful militancy, then, but not for the faint-hearted, for revolution is not without heartache or hardship. It does not come without loss, though it is a reclamation of dignity. The *Ya Basta!* of the Zapatistas, a dignified rage chiming *Enough! Enough! Enough!* The secret is to find the others and begin. Anywhere. Everywhere.

Lines of leakage: The black flag, for life

Not whether we accomplish anarchism today, tomorrow, or within ten centuries, but that we walk towards anarchism today, tomorrow, and always.

(Malatesta 1933: iii)

I like to imagine a different ending, one in which the sense of political impotence projected onto Bernie Sanders is radicalized. Perhaps I am hoping for something like a viral meme of Subcomandante Marcos. No, better yet, an ending where there is no placeholder at all. I like to imagine thousands gathering, raising not another national flag, but the black flag – in mourning of what we have lost and may yet lose, in mourning of the illusions we have clung to, the images of thought we have invested in, the limitations we have placed on the horizon of possibility. Planting the black flag, then, as 'the negation of all flags', as a 'negation of nationhood which puts the human race against itself and denies the unity of all humankind', as a sign of 'anger and outrage at all the hideous crimes against humanity perpetrated in the name of allegiance to one state or another' (Howard Ehrlich 1996). But, also, in recognition of black as the colour of 'germinal existence' – 'an expression of the *élan vital* which marks life as creative', the world as emerging, and reason as arousing from its slumber (Ansell-Pearson 1999: 24). No, liberal representative democracy is *not* the horizon of human possibility after all; it is only one expression. Granted, it has become a dominant expression – one which has overlaid thought, overcoded desire and radically captured and altered material existence. An expression that has given to life a consistency so dense that changing it seems impossible at times. But, as Deleuze, Guattari and anarchist remind us, there are always cracks, lines of drift, lines of leakage and escape. *Germinal life waiting to unfold.*

The question is how to assemble nomadic war machines on lines of flight, how to construct and prefigure alternative ways of being, seeing, hearing, feeling and moving that provide enough consistency to replace the viscosity of the State and capitalism – as well as every other intersecting line of domination, be that racism, patriarchy, class or religion – without becoming either too rigid, so that no experimentation can take place, or too unbridled, destroying the circuits of desire, unbinding the drives and short-circuiting individuation and transindividuation processes. The problem, in other words, is one of care: how to take care of the pharmacological situation, how to take care of each other, how to take care of ourselves and, in this final hour, how to take care of the world. Not according to the capitalist logics of individualism and adaptation that provoke processes of disindividuation, but according to methods of adoption, which is to say processes of individuation and transindividuation that provide a certain amount of consistency and meaning to life, making life feel worth living, giving us reasons to believe in *this* world. It is, from another perspective, a question of becoming-revolutionary, that permanent revolution aimed at the construction of a new body politic that can be sustained through concrete practices which, in turn, continue to effectuate revolutionary conditions. It is a fine balance between the earth and the Cosmos, 'the various entangled lines constituting the "map" of an assemblage (molar lines, molecular lines, lines of flight), and the different relations between the assemblage and the plane of consistency' (*ATP* 512). Deleuze might tell us, in a somewhat different register, that it consists in becoming an apprentice of signs – that which expresses a plurality of worlds, the explication-implication-complication of the fold (*L* 25). 'The sign,' writes Deleuze, 'is the object of an encounter', a violence that compels 'the act of thinking within thought itself' (*P* 62). *A violence. A rupture. A pharmacological situation that is death and life at once.* Hence, we have to take care of the rupture by 'experiencing the violent effect of a sign' *and* then forcing the mind 'to seek the sign's meaning' (*P* 16). That is to say, one has to become affected by the sign, for only 'an affected being can question, which presupposes that it can above all be called into question by its affection' (Stiegler 2013a: 120).

Being capable of being affected has perhaps never been a more difficult a task. With so much complexity to navigate and so few shared practices of meaning to ameliorate the sense of an ending, multitudes opt for 'Netflix and chill' in onesies instead. The fragility of spirit so widely experienced and expressed is itself a sign, in this case of a trauma that has affected – *infected* – 'everything essential in the world', exempting neither body, nor mind (Stiegler 2019: 11). This, then, is the disease of our society according to Stiegler – a widespread disaffection that systemically and systematically disrupts the processes of adoption, the processes of transindividuation which, in turn, eradicates the possibility of posing questions. 'Now, the political question that this raises, beyond merely the metaphysical or psychiatric question', writes Stiegler, 'is how to prevent this nonobject or this *becoming-nothing* of the object (which is necessarily and surely also a becoming-nothing of the subject, *including* the subjectivity of young people, but also of their parents and their offspring) from becoming the *very object of despair*' (Stiegler 2013b: 42).

What I have argued in this book is that bringing together the philosophy of Deleuze and Guattari with the theory and practices of anarchism can help us address this political problem because anarchy, from this perspective, is a politics that acknowledges 'the need to work ourselves out of the present' (Eloff 2019: 21), but *in* the present, in the here and now, in continuous variation and as an 'active experimentation, since we do not know in advance which way a line is going to turn' (*D* 137). It is, then, a throw of the dice, a becoming-worthy of the event by becoming capable of acting, which itself presupposes a becoming capable of being affected. It is nothing short of a noetic act, an encounter with the sign that forces thought within thought, making reasonable that which initially was senseless.

And then they burnt the black flag, the last of them all.

Notes

Chapter 1

1   The term 'statist realism' has been used by Anuradha Dingwaney
    Needham to denote a realist cinematic aesthetic that positions the
    nation-state as its frame of reference. The consequence of this is
    that viewers are assigned a viewing position that places them in
    the position of the nation-state so that their points of view become
    melded. Although this usage of the term coincides to some degree
    with mine, it is less encompassing than the connotations I implicate
    in my application (2011: 86).

2   Although I focus here on European anarchism to make the link to
    Marxism – specifically drawing attention to the fact that they shared
    the same milieu in Europe – and although anarchism is often presented
    as originating in Europe because an early French proponent, Joseph-
    Pierre Proudhon, explicitly called himself an anarchist and coined the
    slogan, 'Anarchy is order; government is civil war', in 1848 from which
    Anselme Bellegarrigue derived the symbolized 'A' in a circle Ⓐ – these
    days frequently found graffitied. This sparked myriad movements
    of people unambiguously organizing themselves around anarchist
    principles, such as anti-statism, anti-capitalism, direct action, mutual
    aid, egalitarianism and decentralized organization, to name a few, who
    also overtly called themselves anarchists. However, anarchism has a
    diverse history that is characterized by movements that were sometimes
    explicitly *anarchist* and sometimes *anarchistic*, meaning they organized
    around the same principles as explicit anarchism. In *African Anarchism*,
    for example, Sam Mbah and I. E. Igariwey detail African practices
    such as self-governing, communalism and healthier relationships with
    the environment which changed dramatically when African countries
    became colonized and capitalized (2001). In the United States, Black
    Anarchic Radicals or 'Anarkatas' can be traced through, for example, the

Black Panther Party (BPP), who were themselves influenced by the work of Malcolm X; the Black Liberation Army (BLA) who challenged racial oppression and capitalism, and the Street Trans* Action Revolutionaries (STAR) who analysed liberation more holistically and participated in numerous anti-war struggles (Afrofuturist Abolitionists of the Americas 2020). Anarchist and anarchistic movements can also be traced to the Philippines, Burma, Tibet, Nepal, South Korea, Japan, China, Taiwan, Thailand, Bangladesh, Indonesia, Algeria and may parts of Latin America, including Uruguay, Bolivia, Argentina, Chile, Antilles, Cuba, Peru, Venezuela, Ecuador, Brazil and Panama. Contemporary and ongoing examples include the well-documented uprising of Zapatistas in the region of Chiapas in Mexico and the Kurdish revolution in Rojava, a northeastern region in Syria – documents of which can be found on the *The Anarchist Library* (https://theanarchistlibrary.org). For more on these histories see this incomplete list:

1. Cappelletti, A. J. (2017), *Anarchism in Latin America*, trans. G. Palmer-Fernández, Oakland, CA: AK Press.
2. Dangl, B. (2019), *The Five Hundred Year Rebellion: Indigenous Movements and the Decolonization of History in Bolivia*, Oakland, CA: AK Press.
3. Dirik, D., D. Levi Strauss, M. Taussig and P. Lamborn Wilson (1970), *To Dare Imagining: Rojava Revolution*, Oakland, CA: AK Press.
4. Henck, N. (2018), *The Zapatistas' Dignified Rage: Final Public Speeches of Subcommander Marcos*, trans. H. Gales, Oakland, CA: AK Press.
5. Katsiaficas, G. (2012), *Asia's Unknown Uprisings Vol. 1: South Korean Social Movements in the 20th Century*, Oakland, CA: PM Press.
6. Katsiaficas, G. (2013), *Asia's Unknown Uprisings Vol. 2: People Power in the Philippines, Burma, Tibet, China, Taiwan, Bangladesh, Nepal, Thailand, and Indonesia, 1947–2009*, Oakland, CA: PM Press.
7. Porter, D. (2011), *Eyes to the South: French Anarchists and Algeria*, Oakland, CA: AK Press.

3   These initial critiques of the State have been complicated over the
    years, especially post-1945. For one, the State and its machinery have
    been linked to white supremacy – rather than just 'race' – by Lorenzo
    Kom'boa Ervin who writes: 'As long as white society, (through the
    State which says it is acting in the name of white people), continues
    to oppress and dominate all the institutions of the Black community,
    racial tension will continue to exist, and whites generally will continue
    to be seen as the enemy' (2016: 17). That is, because the State is at
    its core hierarchical and oppressive, it will, no matter what form of
    government may be in power, no matter what race the person in
    power, continue to produce hierarchical and oppressive relations that
    reproduce whiteness which pits races, like genders, against each other.
    Ervin's critique of the State also points to a flaw in early anarchist
    critiques, which is that they did not take into consideration the full
    scope of the effects of colonialism and racial capitalism. Although I
    have not spent nearly enough time on this subject matter in the current
    book, this is solely because this kind of introductory text does not
    allow sufficient space to deal with what is surely a book-length topic.
    Readers who are interested in the subject may want to refer to Paula
    Chakravartty and Denise Ferreira da Silva's 2012 article, 'Accumulation,
    Dispossession, and Debt: The Racial Logic of Global Capitalism – An
    Introduction', published in *American Quarterly* 64(3): 361–85.

4   To be clear, Marx was critical of the State and granted it relative
    autonomy, but his analysis differed markedly from anarchist analyses
    in that he viewed the State as 'largely derivative of the economic forces
    and class interests' (Newman 2004). Saul Newman explains:

> One of the central debates in Marxist theory has been on
> precisely this question. David Held and Joel Krieger argue that
> there are two main strands in the Marxist theory about the
> relation between classes and the state. The first – let us call it
> (1a) – exemplified by Marx's account of Bonapartism, stresses
> the relative autonomy of the state. It sees state institutions
> and the bureaucracy as constituting a virtually separate site

in society – its logic is not determined by class interests and it assumes a centrality in society. The second strand (2a) which Held and Krieger argue is the dominant one in Marxist thought, sees the state as an instrument of class domination, whose structure and operation are determined by class interests.

(Newman 2004)

Marx, then, pays attention to different forms of State power but does not pay enough attention to it as an *a priori* apparatus of capture and oppression. For a detailed account, see Newman, S. (2004), 'Anarchism, Marxism and the Bonapartist State', *The Anarchist Library*. Available online: https://theanarchistlibrary.org/library/saul-newman-anarchism-marxism-and-the-bonapartist-state (accessed 14 April 2021).

Chapter 2

1   For an excellent overview of Deleuze and Guattari's engagement with Clastres, see Kalyniuk, G. (2019), 'Pierre Clastres and the Amazonian War Machine', in C. Gray van Heerden and A. Eloff (eds), *Deleuze and Anarchism*, 218–36, Edinburgh: Edinburgh University Press.

2   Karl Widerquist and Grant McCall give an excellent overview of how these myths became touchstones in political philosophy in *Prehistoric Myths in Modern Political Philosophy* (2017).

3   In their new book, *The Dawn of Everything*, David Graeber and David Wengrow go to great lengths to show that 'the world of hunter-gatherers as it existed before the coming of agriculture was one of bold social experiments' – at any time as imaginative as contemporary experiments (2021, 4). What makes Graeber and Wengrow's work radical, however, is that the authors argue that Hobbes and Rousseau's notion of the 'state of nature', while commonplace to the contemporary reader, was in fact profound and perturbing in their day, and 'opened new doors of the imagination' (Graeber and Wengrow 2021, 21) because it introduced the idea of an 'egalitarian State of Nature; at least in the minimal sense

of a default state that might be shared by societies which they saw as lacking government, writing, religion, private property or other significant means of distinguishing themselves from one another' (Graeber and Wengrow 2021, 46). This, no less, was a response to 'the indigenous American critique of European society' which 'began as widespread expressions of outrage and distaste' (Graeber and Wengrow 2021, 61) at 'the squabbling, the lack of mutual aid, the blind submission to authority' and 'the organization of private property' which could be converted into power over others (Graeber and Wengrow 2021, 52). The book is a feat and has important implications for political thought and action. I would urge readers to read it alongside this one as I cannot possibly do it justice in a few paragraphs, or even a few pages.

Chapter 3

1 At the time of writing, the Pandora papers were leaked, revealing even more 'secret deals and hidden assets of some of the world's richest and most powerful people' (Guardian investigations team 2021). For more on this, see https://www.theguardian.com/news/2021/oct/03/pandora-papers-biggest-ever-leak-of-offshore-data-exposes-financial-secrets-of-rich-and-powerful.

2 See *The Deleuze Seminars*, available online: https://deleuze.cla.purdue.edu/index.php/seminars/thousand-plateaus-v-state-apparatus-and-war-machines-ii/lecture-06.

3 See *The Deleuze Seminars*, available online: https://deleuze.cla.purdue.edu/index.php/seminars/anti-oedipus-i/lecture-02.

Chapter 4

1 See Klein, N. (2002), *No Logo: Taking Aim at the Brand Bullies*, Toronto: Knopf Canada.

2 Some of the ideas in this chapter were formulated with Aragorn Eloff in Gray, C. and A. Eloff (2021), 'Fabulation in a Time of Algorithmic Ecology: Making the Future Possible Again', in S. Das and A. Roy Pratihar (eds), *Technology, Urban Space and the Networked Community*, 105–33, London: Springer Nature.

3 Yuk Hui remarks that recursion, as it is used here, should be 'distinguished from Gödel's concept of general recursivity or Church's Lambda Calculus' and be thought of rather in terms of the Turing machine which 'went beyond the conceptual recursivity through the exteriorization of reason in concrete and material terms' (2015b: 133).

Chapter 5

1 See https://www.youtube.com/watch?v=yQGqMVuAk04&ab_channel=Quartz.

2 For more on the extension of Guattari's three ecologies to include a fourth, namely algorithmic ecology, see Gray, C. and A. Eloff (forthcoming), 'The Fourth Ecology: Hikikomori, Depressive Hedonia and Algorithmic Ubiquity', in Mirlea Sacks et al. (eds), *Cyber Century (Studies in Online Civilization, Volume 2)*, Maryland: Montagu House.

3 The BwO refers in general to the virtual or preindividual field of undifferentiated 'funds' for the unfolding of being. It is both what gives rise to being and that which continues the development of being through individuation and transindividuation processes, as we saw in Chapter 4. Although the plane of consistency, or the virtual, is undifferentiated, it does have intensities circulating on it. These intensities, in turn, create tensions – or a disparateness between at least two different orders – which function as the primer for individuation processes. The BwO is about *how* to create the right kinds of intensities or, to put it differently, about how to create the right conditions for living a life of intensity that is neither too impassioned – because it leads to burnout – nor too static, because then little is achieved.

Chapter 6

1   Ian McKay presents an excellent analysis of Lenin in this regard. See McKay, I. (2019), 'The State and Revolution: Theory and Practice', *The Anarchist Library*. Available online: https://theanarchistlibrary.org/ library/iain-mckay-anarcho-the-state-and-revolution-theory-and-practice (accessed 27 February 2021).

Bibliography

Abensour, M. (2008), 'Persistent Utopia', *Constellations* 15: 406–21.

Acklesberg, M. A. (2005), *Free Women of Spain: Anarchism and the Struggle for the Emancipation of Women*, Oakland, CA: AK Press.

Afrofuturist Abolitionists of the Americas (2020), 'Mapping Our Legacy: The Narrative of Black Struggle', *The Anarchist Library*. Available online: https://theanarchistlibrary.org/library/anonymous-mapping-our-legacy (accessed 12 January 2021).

Ansell-Pearson, K. (1999), *Germinal Life: The Difference and Repetition of Deleuze*, London and New York: Routledge.

Archibald, M. (2007), 'Atamansha: The Life of Marusya Nikiforova', *The Anarchist Library*. Available online: https://theanarchistlibrary.org/library/malcolm-archibald-atamansha (accessed 14 February 2021).

Austin Anarchist Study Group (2012), 'Our New Names for Alienation', *The Anarchist Library*. Available online: https://theanarchistlibrary.org/library/austin-anarchist-study-group-our-new-names-for-alienation (accessed 3 June 2021).

Baher, Z. (2018), 'Confederalism, Democratic Confederalism and Rojava', *Libcom*, 20 February. Available online: https://libcom.org/library/confederalism-democratic-confederalism-rojava (accessed 5 June 2021).

Bakunin, M. (1926), 'The Capitalist System', *Anarchist Archives*. Available online: http://dwardmac.pitzer.edu/anarchist_archives/bakunin/capstate.html (accessed 21 July 2020).

Bakunin, M. (1953), 'The Immorality of the State', *The Anarchist Library*. Available online: https://theanarchistlibrary.org/library/michail-bakunin-the-immorality-of-the-state (accessed 17 April 2021).

Bakunin, M. (1977a), 'Church and State', in G. Woodcock (ed.), *The Anarchist Reader*, 81–7, Glasgow: Fontana Paperbacks.

Bakunin, M. (1977b), 'Perils of the Marxist State Michael Bakunin', in G. Woodcock (ed.), *The Anarchist Reader*, 140–2, Glasgow: Fontana Paperbacks.

Barclay, H. (2002), *The State*, London: Freedom Press.

Barstow, D., S. Craig and R. Buettner (2018), 'Trump Engaged in Suspect Tax Schemes as He Reaped Riches from His Father', *New York Times*, 2 October. Available online: https://www.nytimes.com/interactive/2018/10/02/us/politics/donald-trump-tax-schemes-fred-trump.html (accessed 15 April 2020).

Berardi, F. (2011), *After the Future*, trans. A. Bove, M. Cooper, E. Empson, Enrico, G. Mecchia and Tiziana Terranova, Oakland, CA: AK Press.

Berkman, A. (1972), *What Is Communist Anarchism?* New York: Dover Publications, Inc.

Biehl, J. (1999), *The Murray Bookchin Reader*, Montréal: Black Rose Books.

Bonanno, A. M. (2009), 'From Riot to Insurrection: Analysis for an Anarchist Perspective against Post-Industrial Capitalism', trans. Jean Weir, *Elephant Editions*. Available online: http://digitalelephant.blogspot.com/2010/08/from-riot-to-insurrection.html (accessed 3 May 2021).

Bookchin, M. (1987), *The Modern Crisis*, Montréal and New York: Black Rose Books.

Bookchin, M. (1993), 'What Is Social Ecology?', *The Anarchist Library*. Available online: https://theanarchistlibrary.org/library/murray-bookchin-what-is-social-ecology-1 (accessed 24 May 2021).

Bookchin, M. (2005), *The Ecology of Freedom: The Emergence and Dissolution of Hierarchy*, Oakland, CA: AK Press.

Bookchin, M. (2016), 'The Bernie Sanders Paradox: When Socialism Grows Old', *Libcom*, 5 October. Available online: https://libcom.org/library/bernie-sanders-paradox-when-socialism-grows-old (accessed 20 January 2020).

Bratton, B. H. (2015), *The Stack: On Software and Sovereignty*, London and Cambridge, MA: MIT Press.

brown, a. m. (2017), *Emergent Strategy: Shaping Change, Changing Worlds*, Oakland, CA: AK Press.

brown, a. m. (2020), *We Will Not Cancel Us*, Oakland, CA: AK Press.

Burrell, J. (2016), 'How the Machine "Thinks": Understanding Opacity in Machine Learning Algorithms', *Big Data & Society* 3(1): 1–12.

Casen, C. (2012), 'Bolivian Katarism: The Emergence of an Indian Challenge to the Social Order', *Critique Internationale*, 57(4): 23–36. https://doi.org/10.3917/crii.057.0023

Clark, J. P. (2009), 'Anarchy and the Dialectic of Utopia', in R. Amster, A. DeLeon, L. A. Fernandez, A. J. Nocella, II and D. Shannon, (eds), *Contemporary Anarchist Studies: An Introductory Anthology of Anarchy in the Academy*, 9–27, London and New York: Routledge.

Clastres, P. (1989), *Society against the State: Essays in Political Anthropology*, trans. R. Hurley and A. Stein, New York: Zone Books.

Clastres, P. (2010), *Archaeology of Violence*, trans. J. Herman, Los Angeles, CA: Semiotext(e).

Colson, D. (2019), *A Little Philosophical Lexicon of Anarchism from Proudhon to Deleuze*, trans. J. Cohn, Colchester and New York: Minor Compositions.

CrimethInc. (n.d.), 'To Change Everything', *CrimethInc*. Available online: https://crimethinc.com/tce (accessed 29 June 2021).

CrimethInc. (2018), 'There Is No Migrant Crisis', *CrimethInc*. Available online: https://crimethinc.com/zines/there-is-no-migrant-crisis (accessed 17 April 2021).

CrimethInc. (2019), '1919: When the Bolsheviks Turned on the Workers', *CrimethInc.*, 12 March. Available online: https://crimethinc.com/2019/03/12/when-the-bolsheviks-turned-on-the-workers-looking-back-on-the-putilov-and-astrakhan-strikes-one-hundred-years-later (accessed 14 February 2021).

Cusicanqui, S. R. (1990), 'Liberal Democracy and *Ayllu* Democracy in Bolivia: The Case of Northern Potosí', *The Journal of Development Studies* 26(4): 97–121, DOI: 10.1080/00220389008422175.

Cusicanqui, S. R. (2009), 'Katarismo and Indigenous Popular Mobilization, Bolivia, 1970s – Present', in I. Ness (ed.), *The International Encyclopedia of Revolution and Protest*, 95–109, New Jersey: Wiley-Blackwell.

Cusicanqui, S. R. (2012), '*Ch'ixinakax utxiwa*: A Reflection on the Practices and Discourses of Decolonization', *The South Atlantic Quarterly* 111(1): 95–109.

Dangl, B. (2019), *The Five Hundred Year Rebellion: Indigenous Movements and the Decolonization of History in Bolivia*, Oakland, CA: AK Press.

De Cleyre, V. (2005), *Exquisite Rebel: The Essays of Voltairine de Cleyre – Feminist, Anarchist, Genius*, eds. S. Presley and C. Sartwell, New York: State University of New York Press.

Deleuze, G. (1988a), *Spinoza: Practical Philosophy*, trans. R. Hurley San, Francisco: City Lights Books.

Deleuze, G. (1988b), *Foucault*, trans. S. Hand, London: Athlone Press.

Deleuze, G. (1989), *Cinema 2: The Time-Image*, trans. H. Tomlinson and R. Galeta, Minneapolis: University of Minnesota Press.

Deleuze, G. (1990), *The Logic of Sense*, trans. M. Lester with C. Stivale, ed. Contantin V. Boundas, New York: Columbia University Press.

Deleuze, G. (1991a), *Empiricism and Subjectivity: An Essay on Hume's Theory of Human Nature*, trans. C. V. Boundas, New York: Columbia University Press.

Deleuze, G. (1991b), *Bergsonism*, trans. Hugh Tomlinson and Barbara Habberjam, New York: Zone Books.

Deleuze, G. (1991c), *Masochism: Coldness and Cruelty*, trans. J. McNeil and A. Willm, New York: Zone Books.

Deleuze, G. (1992a), *Expressionism in Philosophy: Spinoza*, trans. M. Joughin, New York: Zone Books.

Deleuze, G. (1992b), 'Postscript on the Societies of Control', *October* 59: 3–7.

Deleuze, G. (1993), *The Fold: Leibniz and the Baroque*, trans. T. Conley, Minneapolis: University of Minnesota Press.

Deleuze, G. (1994), *Difference and Repetition*, trans. P. Patton, London: Athlone Press.

Deleuze, G. (1997), *Negotiations, 1972–1990*, trans. M. Joughin, New York: Columbia University Press.

Deleuze, G. (2004), *Desert Islands and Other Texts 1953–1974*, trans. M. Taormina, London and Cambridge, MA: MIT Press.

Deleuze, G. (2007), *Two Regimes of Madness: Texts and Interviews 1975–1995*, ed. D. Lapoujade, trans. A. Hodges and M. Taormina, Los Angeles, CA: Semiotext(e).

Deleuze, G. (2008), *Proust and Signs*, trans. R. Howard, London and New York: Continuum.

Deleuze, G. and F. Guattari (1983), *Anti-Oedipus: Capitalism and Schizophrenia*, trans. R. Hurley, M. Seem and H. R. Lane, Minneapolis: Minnesota University Press.

Deleuze, G. and F. Guattari (1986), *Kafka: Toward a Minor Literature*, trans. D. Polan, Minneapolis and London: University of Minnesota Press.

Deleuze, G. and F. Guattari (1987), *A Thousand Plateaus: Capitalism and Schizophrenia*, trans. B. Massumi, London: Continuum.

Deleuze, G. and F. Guattari (1994), 'Capitalism: A Very Special Delirium', in C. Kraus and S. Lotringer (eds), *Hatred of Capitalism*, 215–20, Los Angeles, CA: Semiotext(e).

Deleuze, G. and F. Guattari (1995), *What Is Philosophy*, trans. H. Tomlinson and G. Burchell, New York: Columbia University Press.

Deleuze, G. and C. Parnet (2002), *Dialogues*, trans. Hugh Tomlinson and Barbara Habberjam, New York: Columbia University Press.

Ember, S. (2020), 'Bernie Sanders Drops out of 2020 Democratic Race for President', *New York Times*, 8 April. Available online: https://www.nytimes.com/2020/04/08/us/politics/bernie-sanders-drops-out.html (accessed 30 January 2020).

Ehrlich, H. J. (1996), 'Why the Black Flag?', *The Anarchist Library*. Available online: http://theanarchistlibrary.org/library/howard-j-ehrlich-why-the-black-flag (accessed 1 July 2021).

Eloff, A. (2019), 'Crowned Anarchy-Anarchy-Anarchism – Countereffectuating Deleuze and Guattari's Politics', in C. Gray van Heerden and A. Eloff (eds), *Deleuze and Anarchism*, 11–30, Edinburgh: Edinburgh University Press.

Ervin, L. K. (2016), 'Smash the Right Wing!', *Black Anarchism: A Reader by Black Rose Anarchist Federation*, 29 February. Available online: https://blackrosefed.org/black-anarchism-a-reader/ (accessed 3 February 2020).

Fabbri, L. (1921), 'The Anarchist Concept of the Revolution', *The Anarchist Library*. Available online: https://theanarchistlibrary.org/library/luigi-fabbri-the-anarchist-concept-of-the-revolution (accessed 3 May 2021).

Federici, S. (2018), *Witches, Witch-Hunting and Women*, Oakland, CA: PM Press.

Fisher, M. (2009), *Capitalist Realism: Is There No Alternative?*, Winchester: O Books.

Fitzgibbon, W. and M. Hudson (2021), 'Five Years Later, Panama Papers Still Having a Big Impact', *ICIJ*, 3 April. Available online: https://www.icij.org/investigations/panama-papers/five-years-later-panama-papers-still-having-a-big-impact/ (accessed 14 April 2020).

Foucault, M. (2000), *Power: The Essential Works of Foucault*, ed. James Faubion, trans. R. Hurley, New York: New Press.

Foucault, M. (2008), *The Birth of Biopolitics: Lectures at the Collège de France, 1978–79*, trans. Graham Burchell, New York: Palgrave Macmillan.

Fourcade, M. and K. Healy (2017), 'Seeing Like a Market', *Socio-Economic Review* 15(1): 9–29, DOI: 10.1093/ser/mww033.

Geerts, E. and D. Carstens (2019), 'Ethico-onto-epistemology', *Philosophy Today* 63(4): 915–25, DOI: 10.5840/philtoday202019301.

Gelderloos, P. (2016), *Worshipping Power: An Anarchist View of Early State Formation*, Oakland, CA: AK Press.

Goldman, E. (1996), *Red Emma Speaks: An Emma Goldman Reader*, ed. A. K. Shulman, New York: Humanity Books.

Gordon, U. (2007), 'Anarchism Reloaded', *Journal of Political Ideologies* 12(1): 29–48.

Gordon, U. (2017), 'Prefigurative Politics between Ethical Practice and Absent Promise', *Political Studies* 66(2): 521–37, https://doi.org/10.1177/0032321717722363.

Graeber, D. (2011), *Debt: The First 5,000 Years*, New York: Melville House.

Graeber, D. and D. Wengrow (2021), *The Dawn of Everything: A New History of Humanity*, New York: Farrar, Straus and Giroux.

Gray van Heerden, C. and A. Eloff (2019), *Deleuze and Anarchism*, Edinburgh: Edinburgh University Press.

Guattari, F. (1995), *Chaosmosis: An Ethico-aesthetic Paradigm*, trans. P. Bains and J. Pefanis, Bloomington and Indianapolis: Indiana University Press.

Guattari, F. (1996), *Soft Subversions: Text and Interviews, 1977–1985*, ed. S. Lotringer, trans. C. Wiener and E. Wittman, Los Angeles, CA: Semiotext(e).

Guattari, F. (2000), *The Three Ecologies*, trans. I. Pindar and P. Sutton, London: The Athlone Press.

Guattari, F. (2006), *The Anti-Oedipus Papers*, ed. S. Nadaud, trans. K. Gotman, Los Angeles, CA: Semiotext(e).

Guattari, F. (2013), *Schizoanalytic Cartographies*, trans. A. Goffey, London: Bloomsbury Academic.

Guattari, F. (2015), *Psychoanalysis and Transversality: Texts and Interviews 1955–1971*, trans. A. Hodges, Los Angeles, CA: Semiotext(e).

Guattari, F. (2016), *Lines of Flight: For Another World of Possibilities*, trans. A. Goffey, London and New York: Bloomsbury.

Guattari, F. and S. Rolnik (2008), *Molecular Revolution in Brazil*, trans. K. Clapshow and B. Holmes, Los Angeles, CA: Semiotext(e).

Harding, L. (2016), 'What Are the Panama Papers? A Guide to History's Biggest Data Leak', *Guardian*, 5 April. Available online: https://www.theguardian.com/news/2016/apr/03/what-you-need-to-know-about-the-panama-papers (accessed 14 April 2020).

Hartman, S. (2006), *Lose Your Mother: A Journey along the Atlantic Slave Route*, New York: Farrar, Straus and Giroux.

Holloway, J. (2005), 'The Concept of Power and the Zapatistas', *Libcom*, 1 November. Available online: https://libcom.org/library/concept-power-zapatistas-john-holloway (accessed 4 July 2021).

Holloway, J. (2010), *Crack Capitalism*, London and New York: Pluto Press.

Holloway, J. (2011), 'Zapatismo', *John Holloway*, 30 July. Available online: http://www.johnholloway.com.mx/2011/07/30/zapatismo/ (accessed 3 July 2021).

Hui, Y. (2015a), 'Modulation after Control', *New Formations* 84(84–5): 74–91.

Hui, Y. (2015b), 'Algorithmic Catastrophe – The Revenge of Contingency', *Parrhesia* 23: 122–43.

Hui, Y. (2018), 'Archives of the Future: Remarks on the Concept of Tertiary Protention', in Karl-Magnus Johansson (ed.), *Inscription*, 129–151, Göteborg: Landsarkivet i Göteborg.

Husserl, E. (1991), 'On the Phenomenology of the Consciousness of Internal Time (1893–1917)', in *Collected Works, vol. 4*, trans. J. Brough, Dordrecht: Kluwer Academic Publishers.

Internationalist Commune of Rojava (2018), *Make Rojava Green Again: Building an Ecological Society*, Bristol: Dog Section Press.

Jun N. (2012), *Anarchism and Political Modernity*, London and New York: Continuum.

Jun, N. J. (2019), 'The State', in C. Levy and M. S. Adams (eds), *The Palgrave Handbook of Anarchism*, 27–46, London: Palgrave Macmillan.

Kalpokas, I. (2019), *Algorithmics Governance: Politics in the Post-Human Era*, Switzerland: Palgrave Macmillan.

Kinna, R. (2005), *Anarchism: A Beginner's Guide*, Oxford: Oneworld.

Kinna, R. (2016), 'Utopianism and Prefiguration', in S. D. Chrostowska and J. D. Ingram (eds), *Political Uses of Utopia: New Marxist, Anarchist, and Radical Democratic Perspectives*, 198–215, New York: Columbia University Press.

Koopman, C. (2018), 'Infopolitics, Biopolitics, Anatomopolitics: Toward a Genealogy of the Power of Data', *Graduate Faculty Philosophy Journal* 39(1): 103–28, https://doi.org/10.5840/gfpj20183914.

Krisis Group (2017), 'Manifesto against Labour', *Libcom*, 28 May. Available online: https://libcom.org/library/manifesto-against-labour-krisis-group (accessed 4 March 2020).

Kropotkin, P. (1892), 'Revolutionary Studies', *The Anarchist Library*. Available online: https://theanarchistlibrary.org/library/petr-kropotkin-revolutionary-studies (accessed 3 May 2021).

Kropotkin, P. (1896), 'The State: Its Historic Role', *The Anarchist Library*. Available online: https://theanarchistlibrary.org/library/petr-kropotkin-the-state-its-historic-role (accessed 17 April 2021).

Kropotkin, P. A. (1943), *The State: Its Historic Role*, London: Freedom Press.

Kropotkin, P. A. (1970), *Selected Writings on Anarchism and Revolution*, Massachusetts and London: MIT Press.

Kropotkin, P. A. (2005), *The Conquest of Bread and Other Writings*, ed. M. Shatz, Cambridge: Cambridge University Press.

Landauer, G. (1978), *For Socialism*, St. Louis: Telos Press.

Landauer, G. (2005), 'Destroying the State by Creating Socialism', in R. Graham (ed.), *Anarchism: A Documentary History of Libertarian Ideas, Vol. 1, from Anarchy to Anarchism (300 CE To 1939)*, 164–166, Montréal: Black Rose Books.

Landstreicher, W. (2009), *Willful Disobedience*, San Francisco: Ardent Press.

Laurson, E. (2021), *The Operating System: An Anarchist Theory of the Modern State* [E-reader version], Oakland, CA: AK Press.

Lennard, N. (2019), *Being Numerous: Essays on Non-Fascist Life*, London and New York: Verso.

Lovink, G. (2019), 'Cybernetics for the Twenty-First Century: An Interview with Philosopher Yuk Hui', *e-flux* 102. Available online: https://www.e-flux.com/journal/102/282271/cybernetics-for-the-twenty-first-century-an-interview-with-philosopher-yuk-hui/ (accessed 30 November 2021).

Malatesta, E. (1922), 'Revolution in Practice', *The Anarchist Library*. Available online: https://theanarchistlibrary.org/library/errico-malatesta-revolution-in-practice (accessed 7 May 2021).

Malatesta, E. (1933), *A Talk between Two Workers*, Oakland, CA: Man!

Malatesta, E. (1995), *The Anarchist Revolution: Polemical Articles 1924–1931*, ed. V. Richards, London: Freedom Press.

Marcos, S. (2004), *Ya Basta!: Ten Years of the Zapatista Uprising*, ed. Žiga Vodovnik, Oakland, CA: AK Press.

Marcos, S. (2006), *The Other Campaign/La Otra Campaña*, San Francisco: City Lights Books.

Martin, R. (2015), *Knowledge LTD: Towards a Social Logic of the Derivative*, Philadelphia, PA: Temple University Press.

Marx, K. (1973), *Grundrisse: Foundations of the Critique of Political Economy (Rough Draft)*, trans. M. Nicolaus, London: Penguin Books in association with New Left Review.

May, T. (1994), *The Political Philosophy of Poststructuralist Anarchism*, University Park: Pennsylvania State University Press.

Mbah, S. and I. E. Igariwey (2001), 'African Anarchism: The History of a Movement', *The Anarchist Library*. Available online: https://theanarchistlibrary.org/library/sam-mbah-i-e-igariwey-african-anarchism-the-history-of-a-movement (accessed 22 July 2020).

McQuillan, D. (2020), 'Deep Bureaucracy and Autonomist AI', in M. Hlavajova and S. Lutticken (eds), *Deserting from the Culture Wars*, 227–42, Cambridge, MA: MIT Press.

Milstein, C. (2000), 'Reclaim the Cities: From Protest to Popular Power', *The Anarchist Library*. Available online: https://theanarchistlibrary.org/library/cindy-milstein-reclaim-the-cities-from-protest-to-popular-power.a4.pdf (accessed 5 April 2021).

Milstein, C. (2010), *Anarchism and Its Aspirations*, Oakland, CA: AK Press/The Institute for Anarchist Studies.

Montgomery, N. and C. bergman (2017), *Joyful Militancy: Building Resistance in Toxic Times*, Oakland, CA: AK Press.

Morgan, L. H. (1877), *Ancient Society; Or: Researches in the Lines of Human Progress from Savagery through Barbarism to Civilization*, New York: H. Holt.

Moulier-Boutang, Y. (2012), *Cognitive Capitalism*, Cambridge: Polity Press.

Nail, T. (2010), 'Constructivism and the Future Anterior of Radical Politics', *Anarchist Developments in Cultural Studies* 1: 73–94.

Nail, T. (2012), *Returning to Revolution: Deleuze, Guattari and Zapatismo*, Edinburgh: Edinburgh University Press.

Nappalos, S. N. (2019), *Emergence and Anarchism: A Philosophy of Power, Action, and Liberation*, Oakland, CA: AK Press.

Needham, A. D. (2011), 'Statist Realism and Its Discontents: Another Optics for Shyam Benegal's *Ankur* (*The Seedling*, 1973)', *South Asian Review* 32 (1): 185–212, DOI: 10.1080/02759527.2011.11932819.

Newman, S. (2003), 'Empiricism, Pluralism and Politics in Deleuze and Stirner', *The Anarchist Library*. Available online: https://theanarchistlibrary.org/library/saul-newman-empiricism-pluralism-politics-deleuze-and-stirner (accessed 29 June 2021).

Newman, S. (2006), 'Anarchism and the Politics of Ressentiment', *Libcom*, 11 September. Available online: http://libcom.org/library/anarchism-and-the-politics-of-ressentiment-saul-newman (accessed 17 April 2021).

Newman, S. (2010a), *The Politics of Postanarchism*, Edinburgh: Edinburgh University Press.

Newman, S. (2010b), 'Voluntary Servitude Reconsidered: Radical Politics and the Problem of Self-Domination', *The Anarchist Library*. Available online: https://theanarchistlibrary.org/library/saul-newman-voluntary-servitude-reconsidered-radical-politics-and-the-problem-of-self-dominatio (accessed 22 April 2021).

Nietzsche, F. (1974), *The Gay Science*, trans. W. Kaufmann, New York: Vintage Books.

Noble, S. U. (2018), *Algorithms of Oppression: How Search Engines Reinforce Racism*, New York: New York University Press.

Parsons, L. (2004), *Freedom, Equality & Solidarity: Writings & Speeches, 1878–1937*, ed. G. Ahrens, Chicago: Charles H. Kerr.

Parsons, L. (2016), 'The Principles of Anarchism', *Black Anarchism: A Reader by Black Rose Anarchist Federation*, 29 February. Available online: https://blackrosefed.org/black-anarchism-a-reader/ (accessed 3 February 2020).

Pasquale, F. (2015), *The Black Box Society: The Secret Algorithms That Control Money and Information*, Cambridge, MA: Harvard University Press.

Protevi, J. (2019), *Edges of the State*, Minneapolis and London: University of Minnesota Press.

Proudhon, P.-J. (1848), 'Toast to the Revolution', *The Anarchist Library*. Available online: https://theanarchistlibrary.org/library/pierre-joseph-proudhon-toast-to-the-revolution (accessed 7 May 2021).

Proudhon, J.-P. (1851), 'The General Idea of the Revolution in the 19th Century', *The Anarchist Library*. Available online: https://theanarchistlibrary.org/library/pierre-joseph-proudhon-the-general-idea-of-the-revolution-in-the-19th-century (accessed 17 April 2021).

Proudhon, P.-J. (1969), *General Idea of the Revolution in the Nineteenth Century*, trans. J. B. Robinson, New York: Haskell House Publishers Ltd.

Proudhon, P.-J. (2012), *The Philosophy of Poverty: The System of Economic Contradictions*, Auckland: The Floating Press.

Raekstad, P. and S. Gradin (2019), *Prefigurative Politics: Building Tomorrow Today*, Cambridge: Polity.

Rancière, J. (2006), *Hatred of Democracy*, London and New York: Verso.

Rouvroy, A. (2011), 'Technology, Virtuality and Utopia: Governmentality in an Age of Autonomic Computing', in M. Hildebrandt and A. Rouvroy (eds), *Law, Human Agency and Autonomic Computing: The Philosophy of Law Meets the Philosophy of Technology*, 119–40, London and New York: Routledge.

Rouvroy, A. and T. Berns (2013), 'Algorithmic Governmentality and Prospects of Emancipation. Disparateness as a Precondition for Individuation through Relationships?', *Réseaux* 177(1): 163–96, DOI: 10.3917/res.177.0163.

Rouvroy, A. and B. Stiegler (2016), 'The Digital Regime of Truth: From the Algorithmic Governmentality to a New Rule of Law', *La Deleuziana* 3: 6–29.

Roy, A. (2016), *The End of Imagination*, Chicago: Haymarket Books.

Sahlins, M. (2017), *Stone Age Economics*, London and New York: Routledge.

Scott, J. C. (1998), *Seeing Like a State: How Certain Schemes to Improve the Human Condition Have Failed*, New Haven and London: Yale University Press.

Scott, J. C. (2009), *The Art of Not Being Governed: An Anarchist History of Upland Southeast Asia*, New Haven: Yale University Press.

Scott, J. C. (2017), *Against the Grain: A Deep History of the Earliest States*, New Haven and London: Yale University Press.

Seyferth, P. (2009), 'Anarchism and Utopia', in R. Amster, A. DeLeon, L. A. Fernandez, A. J. Nocella, II and D. Shannon, (eds), *Contemporary Anarchist Studies: An Introductory Anthology of Anarchy in the Academy*, 280–9, London and New York: Routledge.

Shannon, D. (2012), 'Chopping Off the Invisible Hand: Internal Problems with Markets and Anarchist Theory, Strategy, and Vision', in D. Shannon, A. J. Nocella II and J. Asimakopoulos (eds), *The Accumulation of Freedom: Writings on Anarchist Economics*, 276–90, Oakland, CA: AK Press.

Shannon, D., A. J. Nocella, II and J. Asimakopoulos (2012), 'Anarchist Economics: A Holistic View', in D. Shannon, A. J. Nocella II and J. Asimakopoulos (eds), *The Accumulation of Freedom: Writings on Anarchist Economics*, 11–39, Oakland, CA: AK Press.

Simondon, G. (1992), 'The Genesis of the Individual', in J. Crary and S. Kwinter (eds), *Incorporations*, 297–319, New York: Zone Books.

Simondon, G. (2009), 'The Position of the Problem of Ontogenesis', *Parrhesia* 7: 4–16.

Simondon, G. (2017), *On the Mode of Existence of Technical Objects*, Minneapolis: Univocal.

Smith, A. (1976), *An Inquiry into the Nature and Causes of the Wealth of Nations*, Indianapolis: Liberty Classics.

Spannons, C. (2012), 'Examining the History of Anarchist Economics to See the Future', in D. Shannon, A. J. Nocella II and J. Asimakopoulos (eds), *The Accumulation of Freedom: Writings on Anarchist Economics*, 42–63, Oakland, CA: AK Press.

Srnicek, N. (2016), *Platform Capitalism*, Cambridge: Polity Press.

Starr, A., M. E. Martínez-Torres and P. Rosset (2011), 'A Second Look at Latin American Social Movements', *Latin American Perspectives* 38(1): 102–19.

Stiegler, B. (2006), 'Anamnesis and Hypomnesis: The Memories of Desire', *Ars Industrialis*, 8 April. Available online: https://arsindustrialis.org/anamnesis-and-hypomnesis (accessed 14 August 2020).

Stiegler, B. (2013a), *What Makes Life Worth Living? On Pharmacology*, Cambridge: Polity Press.

Stiegler, B. (2013b), *Uncontrollable Societies of Disaffected Individuals*, trans. D. Ross, Cambridge: Polity Press.

Stiegler, B. (2016), *Automatic Society Volume 1: The Future of Work*, trans. D. Ross, Cambridge: Polity Press.

Stiegler, B. (2019), *The Age of Disruption: Technology and Madness in Computational Capitalism*, trans. D. Ross, Cambridge: Polity Press.

Stiegler, B. (2018), *The Neganthropocene*, trans. D. Ross, Cambridge and London: Open Humanities Press.

Stiegler, B. and I. Rogoff (2010), 'Transindividuation', *e-flux* 14. Available online: https://www.e-flux.com/journal/14/61314/transindividuation/ (accessed 14 June 2020).

Stiglitz, J. E. and M. Pieth (2016), 'Overcoming the Shadow Economy', *Global Policy and Development of the Friedrich-Ebert-Stiftung*, November. Available online: https://library.fes.de/pdf-files/iez/12922.pdf (accessed 14 April 2020).

Stirner, M. (1995), *The Ego and Its Own*, Cambridge: Cambridge University Press.

The Free Association (2010), *Moments of Excess: Movements, Protests and Everyday Life*, Oakland, CA: PM Press.

The Invisible Committee (2009), *The Coming Insurrection*, Los Angeles, CA: Semiotext(e).

Tiqqun (2020), *The Cybernetic Hypothesis*, trans. R. Hurley, Los Angeles, CA: Semiotext(e).

Vasileva, E. (2019), 'Immanent Ethics and Forms of Representation', in C. Gray van Heerden and A. Eloff (eds), *Deleuze and Anarchism*, 103–19, Edinburgh: Edinburgh University Press.

Virilio, P. (2005), *The Original Accident*, Cambridge: Polity Press.

Viveiros de Castro, E. (2010), 'Introduction', in P. Clastres, *Archaeology of Violence*, trans. Jeanine Herman, 9–51, Los Angeles, CA: Semiotext(e).

Volcano, A. and D. Shannon (2012), 'Capitalism in the 2000s: Some Broad Strokes for Beginners', in D. Shannon, A. J. Nocella, II and J. Asimakopoulos (eds), *The Accumulation of Freedom: Writings on Anarchist Economics*, 80–94, Oakland, CA: AK Press.

Wark, M. (2004), *A Hacker Manifesto*, Cambridge, MA, and London: Harvard University Press.

Wark, M. (2015), 'The Vectoralist Class', *e-flux* 65. Available online: https://www.e-flux.com/journal/65/336347/the-vectoralist-class/ (accessed 11 June 2021).

Wark, M. (2019), *Capital Is Dead*, London and New York: Verso.

Wark, M. (2020), *Sensoria: Thinkers for the Twenty-First Century*, London and New York: Verso.

Weiser, M. (1991), 'The Computer for the Twenty- First Century', *Scientific American*, September, 94–100.

Wengrow, D. and D. Graeber (2015), 'Farewell to the "Childhood of Man": Ritual, Seasonality, and the Origins of Inequality', *Journal of the Royal Anthropological Institute* 21(3): 597–619.

Widerquist, K. and G. McCall (2017), *Prehistoric Myths in Modern Political Philosophy*, Edinburgh: Edinburgh University Press.

Williams, C. C. (2005), *A Commodified World? Mapping the Limits of Capitalism*, London: Zed Books.

Woodcock, G. (1977), 'The Tyranny of the Clock', in G. Woodcock (ed.), *The Anarchist Reader*, 132–6, Glasgow: Fontana Paperbacks.

Zuboff, S. (2019), *The Age of Surveillance Capitalism: A Fight for a Human Future at the New Frontier of Power*, New York: Public Affairs.

Index

A

Abdullah Öcalan 55
Adam Smith 60, 71
adapt 78
   adaptation 81, 84, 104, 118, 143, 150
   adapted 18, 103
   adapting 78
   adaptive 15, 103, 105
adopt
   adopted 18, 21, 52, 73, 103, 132
   adopting 103
   adoption 49, 102, 105, 106, 111, 114, 122, 143, 150, 151
   adoptive 114
   adopts 91, 132
affect 29, 70, 103, 105, 122, 134, 135
   affected 103, 105, 122, 135, 142, 151, 152
   affecting 107
   affection 105, 151
   affective 9, 102, 104, 112, 113, 114, 115, 123, 131
   affects 47, 51, 82, 133, 135, 145
affirm 32, 112, 119, 120, 121, 122, 133
   affirmation 104, 119, 120, 123, 124, 140
   affirmed 102, 121, 122
   affirming 9, 103, 110, 115, 119, 120, 142
Alexander Berkman 65
algorithm 107, 107
   algorithmic 2, 6, 7, 75, 83, 84, 86, 87, 90, 91, 93, 94, 95, 107, 116, 122, 138, 142, 158
   algorithmically 84, 90
   algorithms 6, 7, 75, 78, 79, 83, 86, 116

algorithmic governmentality 83, 87
alien
   alienable 64
   alienated 4, 64, 65, 67
   alienating 29, 65
   alienation 4, 36, 64, 65, 66, 68, 69, 70, 74, 92, 95
analogy 16
anti-capitalism 19, 153
anti-production 68, 69
anti-statism 19, 153
   anti-statist 19
apparatus 5, 15, 17, 20, 21, 25, 27, 28, 29, 30, 31, 36, 40, 43, 44, 46, 47, 49, 52, 53, 56, 60, 61, 63, 64, 66, 69, 74, 86, 120, 129, 130, 131, 132, 134, 156
   apparatuses 25, 28, 84
apparatus of capture 21, 30, 36, 43, 44, 46, 49, 53, 56, 60, 61, 63, 64, 74, 130, 156
apprentice 1, 150
   apprenticeship 3, 9, 139
axiom 30, 37, 43
   axiomatic 5, 17, 18, 36, 53, 75
   axiomatically 23
   axiomaticians 32
   axiomatics 31, 32, 33, 35, 37, 39, 41, 43, 45, 47, 49, 51, 53, 55
   axioms 5, 20, 32, 37, 74

B

Bakunin (Mikail) 20, 44, 45, 71
barter 60, 61, 62
becoming-imperceptible 145
becoming-revolutionary 136, 142, 145, 150
Bernie Sanders 11, 12, 13, 14, 18, 149

Body without Organs / BwO 99, 110, 111, 112, 158
Bookchin (Murray) 7, 13, 21, 54, 96, 97

C
cadastral map 48, 49, 63
capitalism 2, 3, 4, 5, 8, 14, 19, 20, 23, 24, 27, 28, 30, 39, 53, 57, 63, 64, 65, 66, 67, 70, 71, 72, 73, 74, 75, 80, 82, 83, 85, 87, 88, 98, 113, 117, 119, 137, 138, 139, 142, 143, 144, 150, 154, 155
    capitalist 4, 14, 15, 22, 23, 24, 26, 27, 28, 39, 57, 64, 66, 67, 68, 69, 70, 72, 74, 75, 95, 137, 140, 150
    capitalist realism 14, 15
    capitalists 69, 85
capture 5, 21, 27, 30, 33, 36, 37, 40, 43, 44, 46, 49, 50, 52, 53, 56, 59, 60, 61, 63, 64, 74, 83, 84, 130, 156
    captured 11, 13, 34, 47, 50, 60, 61, 149
    captures 21, 23, 31, 46, 52, 60, 61, 74
    capturing 21, 50, 54
care 1, 7, 8, 28, 48, 94, 97, 99, 103, 110, 111, 114, 115, 116, 119, 120, 121, 123, 143, 144, 150, 151
    cares 102
    caring 1
class 2, 7, 20, 26, 46, 68, 69, 70, 71, 72, 80, 85, 86, 96, 150, 155, 156
    classes 51, 65, 85, 86, 155
code 82
    coded 25, 28, 42, 102
    codes 25, 26, 47, 64, 87, 131
    coding 25, 27, 38
commodify
    commodification 82

commodified 57
commodity 65, 66, 82
    commodities 26, 28, 31, 46, 82
common 16, 91, 92, 109, 132, 137, 139
consistence 143
    consistencies 103
    consistency 6, 9, 25, 42, 47, 93, 99, 102, 103, 106, 108, 109, 110, 111, 112, 114, 119, 137, 138, 139, 141, 143, 150, 158
    consistent 16, 115, 140, 142, 146
contingence
    contingency 15, 20, 80, 87, 120, 132
    contingent 4, 21, 43, 46, 53, 109
counter-actualize
    counter-actualization 105, 106, 112, 114, 117, 118, 119, 123, 124
    counter-actualizes 105

D
data 18, 75, 78, 82, 83, 84, 85, 86, 87, 88, 98, 101
    database 58
David Graeber 4, 26, 40, 41, 43, 59, 156
debt 7, 25, 26, 27, 52, 60, 61, 62, 63, 76, 80, 155, 165
    debts 62
decode
    decoded 75
    decoding 25, 27, 30, 79, 80, 82
depressive hedonia 14, 122, 158
derivative 82, 155
    derivatively 84
    derivatives 7, 85, 87, 88
    derivatization 87
desire 8, 19, 22, 23, 24, 25, 26, 27, 28, 29, 30, 31, 41, 42, 57, 60, 63, 67, 68, 69, 70, 74, 88, 92, 96, 104, 110, 111, 116, 133, 135, 141, 142, 143, 149, 150

desires 20, 21, 23, 26, 28, 40, 41,
    65, 68, 90, 138, 143, 144
desiring-machine 69
desiring-machines 68, 99, 143
desiring-production 23, 67, 68
deterritorialize
    deterritorialization 50, 79, 80, 82,
        110, 131, 133
    deterritorialized 4, 75, 128
    deterritorializes 131
    deterritorializing 27, 47, 131
diagram 116, 128, 130
    diagrammatic 116, 117, 141
    diagramming 84
    diagrams 87
diagrammatism 136
difference 15, 16, 17, 24, 26, 57, 81,
    85, 114, 137
    differenciated 121
    differenciation 114, 121
different 3, 18, 21, 22, 24, 26, 30, 42,
    52, 54, 63, 65, 66, 74, 94, 104,
    109, 113, 121, 123, 125, 130,
    138, 141, 149, 150, 156, 158
    differentiated 143
    differentiates 19
    differentiation 133
digital 6, 84, 86, 90, 92, 98, 101
digitize
    digitization 6, 75
    digitized 81, 84, 85, 91
direct action 96, 109, 153
disaffect
    disaffected 92, 103, 105, 122
    disaffection 151
disindividuation 92, 150
disparate 7, 48, 70, 81, 107
    disparateness 81, 95, 158
    disparation 81, 95, 106, 108
    disparity 2, 59
dividual 82, 83
dividuation 93
division of labour 65, 71
dogmatic image of thought 4, 15, 16,
    17, 23, 30, 31, 50, 105

dominant 52, 75, 76, 98, 112, 139,
    149, 156
dominate 39, 155
    dominated 55, 146
    dominates 31
    dominating 98
    domination 1, 7, 8, 19, 57, 65, 70,
        71, 72, 73, 96, 108, 113, 119,
        145, 150, 156
    dominations 70
drive 104
    drives 88, 92, 99, 110, 111, 113,
        118, 119, 122, 123, 133, 143,
        150
    driving 23, 42, 63, 68

E
ecosophy 7, 93, 94, 95, 96
    ecosophical 95
emergent strategy 132, 133, 147
Emma Goldman 29, 72
eternal return 106, 107, 117, 119
event 2, 103, 107, 114, 115, 117, 120,
    121, 121, 135, 141, 142, 144,
    145, 146, 152
    events 107, 108, 117, 127, 137
experiment 2, 79, 98, 116, 142
    experimental 109
    experimentation 8, 9, 99, 103,
        108, 109, 110, 111, 112, 114,
        119, 123, 146, 150, 151
    experimentations 9
    experimenting 137
    experiments 14, 128, 156
externalized memory 89, 91

F
fabulates 106, 136
    fabulating III, 8, 9, 22, 136
    fabulation 94, 95, 99, 105, 158
    fabulative 94
faciality 50, 145
    facialization 71
    facializations 145
    facializing 72

Foucault (Michel) 15, 21, 31, 52, 69, 71, 80, 87, 116, 139

G
gender 3, 70, 72, 131, 141
   gendered 30, 72, 145
   genders 155
good 11, 16, 18, 24, 39, 54, 88, 93, 107, 114, 137, 141, 142
good-government 54
govern 20, 38, 42, 43, 132
   governance 75, 83, 87
   governed 19, 31, 33
   governing 83
   governs 83
government 13, 18, 20, 29, 35, 44, 46, 54, 65, 82, 125, 126, 141, 153, 155, 157
   governments 8, 31, 47, 73
governmental 54
   governmentality 6, 7, 21, 52, 68, 69, 71, 73, 75, 76, 83, 87, 88
grammatization 89, 90, 91, 123

H
hack 85, 98
   hacker 85, 86, 88, 98
   hacking VII, 2, 77, 78, 79, 81, 83, 84, 85, 86, 87, 89, 91, 93, 95, 97, 98, 99
hacker classes 85
Harold Barclay 41
hierarchy 19, 70, 73
   hierarchical 7, 21, 24, 63, 65, 66, 96, 109, 132, 155
   hierarchically 74
   hierarchies 46
   hierarchized 53
   hierarchizing 15
hyper-control 80, 81, 82, 83, 84, 89

I
identity 16, 35, 116, 143, 144, 145
   identities 5, 37

image of thought 4, 15, 16, 17, 18, 21, 23, 23, 26, 30, 31, 42, 50, 60, 104, 105, 117, 118, 123
indigenous 33, 34, 35, 36, 38, 42, 73, 140, 154, 157
individualize
   individualization 92, 93, 122
   individualized 67, 86, 144
individuate 92
   individuating 114
individuation 69, 81, 90, 91, 92, 93, 95, 103, 105, 106, 107, 108, 109, 110, 113, 121, 122, 123, 141, 147, 150, 158
infopolitics 83, 87
infopower 87
information 16, 59, 79, 81, 82, 83, 84, 85, 86, 90, 98, 120, 132, 139
inscription 6, 25, 26, 27, 28, 68, 86, 119, 132
   inscriptions 86
instrumentarianism 88
intensity 70, 130, 146, 158
   intensities 99, 103, 105, 107, 110, 111, 115, 117, 121, 123, 128, 137, 141, 143, 147, 158
interpassivity 14

J
James Scott 4, 39, 41
joyful militancy 134, 147

K
knowledge production 18
Kropotkin (Peter) 20, 21, 44, 71, 135, 136, 137
Kurdish Freedom Movement 54–55, 96

L
learn 1, 79, 98, 115, 120
   learning 7, 18, 110, 116, 122, 127, 134, 135
legible 51
   legibility 7, 47, 48, 50, 63, 84

libidinal economy 22, 88
lines of flight 128
logic 16, 17, 38, 41, 51, 52, 60, 63, 65,
    80, 88, 97, 131, 132, 133, 155,
    156
  logics 5, 6, 15, 29, 30, 31, 36, 37,
    42, 47, 49, 50, 61, 65, 70, 71,
    74, 80, 89, 131, 141, 150
logics of enclosure 61
long circuits 89, 91, 92, 93, 94, 95, 96,
    98, 99, 103, 111, 112, 113, 119,
    123, 133, 137
Lucy Parsons 72

M

machine 1, 7, 18, 25, 27, 28, 37, 40,
    64, 76, 84, 124, 129, 130, 131,
    132, 133, 134, 137, 138, 141,
    146, 156, 158
  machined 22, 24, 25, 67
  machinery 27, 29, 30, 43, 155
  machines 20, 67, 68, 69, 70, 80,
    140, 146, 150
  machinic 7, 8, 64, 70, 99
  machining 28
machinic enslavement 64
Maria Nikiforova (Marusya) 126, 127
Mark Fisher 2, 14, 59, 122
Marshall Sahlins 39
Marx (Karl) 6, 20, 24, 40, 64, 65, 66,
    67, 68, 69, 70, 71, 72, 76, 85,
    86, 155, 156
Marxism 20, 153, 156
  Marxist 4, 20, 155, 156
  Marxists 24, 53
metastable 81, 84, 106, 109
  metastability 80, 103, 108
  metastabilization 93
  metastabilized 91
microfascism 29, 31, 121
  microfascisms 143
missing people 95
modulate 27
  modulated 27

modulates 91
modulation 52, 80, 81, 83, 84,
    138, 138
molar 2, 31, 70, 131, 136, 143, 150
molecule
  molecular 29, 31, 70, 96, 136, 142,
    143, 146, 150
  molecules 31
moments of excess 70, 108, 115, 121,
    125, 146
monetary inscription 28
multiplicity 16, 117, 121, 146
  multiplicities 107, 109, 117, 121,
    143, 146
mutual aid 44, 115, 123, 153, 157

N

necessary 4, 5, 15, 17, 21, 37, 43, 45,
    46, 50, 51, 53, 89, 136, 137,
    138, 140
Nestor Mahkno 126, 127, 129
nomad
  nomadic 40, 124, 129, 130, 131,
    132, 133, 134, 137, 138, 146,
    150
  nomadism 37, 49
nomadic war machine 40, 124, 129,
    130, 131, 132, 133, 134, 137,
    138, 146
Nomadology 130
nonstate 24, 25, 28, 38, 39, 41, 42, 43
  nonstatism 40, 130
nonstate societies / stateless societies
    25, 28, 38, 39, 41, 42, 43, 45, 62

O

ontogenesis 81
  ontogenetic 81, 109, 117
opposition 16, 19, 35, 46
  oppositions 51
order-words 139
overcode 26, 64, 131
  overcoded 26, 28, 50, 133, 139,
    149

overcodes 23, 47, 64
overcoding 25, 26, 27, 30, 38, 47,
    50, 61, 68, 74, 132

P

people-to-come 2, 118
Peter Gelderloos 41
Pharmacology 93, 94, 105
pharmacological 77, 93, 102, 103,
    104, 107, 108, 112, 114, 115,
    116, 117, 118, 119, 122, 123,
    142, 150, 151
pharmacologically 110
pharmakon 7, 28, 92, 94, 102, 103,
    110, 113, 115, 120
pharmaka 25, 94, 143
Pierre Clastres 4, 40, 156
power 5, 9, 19, 20, 21, 27, 29, 30, 31,
    33, 37, 38, 41, 42, 44, 45, 46,
    47, 48, 49, 52, 54, 57, 67, 68,
    69, 70, 73, 76, 77, 78, 79, 85,
    87, 88, 104, 105, 112, 114, 115,
    116, 125, 126, 128, 133, 139,
    143, 146, 154, 155, 156, 157
power-holders 49
powered 79
powerful 114, 157
powers 26, 128, 133
prefigure 42, 111, 135, 150
prefigural 19
prefiguration 8, 99, 106, 108, 109,
    110, 111, 112, 113, 118, 123,
    135
prefigurative 110, 111, 112, 114,
    118, 134
prefigures 122, 145
prefiguring 8, 103, 118, 143
primitive accumulation 24, 63, 64,
    79
problem 4, 7, 16, 18, 19, 23, 29, 36,
    48, 63, 67, 78, 83, 84, 94, 98,
    99, 102, 103, 106, 107, 108,
    121, 122, 136, 137, 140, 150,
    151

problematic 95, 109, 121, 147
problématique 94
problematized 32
problems 6, 9, 18, 22, 39, 94, 98,
    99, 105, 106, 107, 112, 114,
    118, 121, 135, 136, 142
profit 8, 13, 27, 46, 49, 50, 51, 54, 56,
    59, 60, 61, 74, 79, 97
profitable 60
proletarianization 89, 90, 91, 123
protention 90, 91, 92, 99, 104, 119
protentional 111, 114, 119
protentions 90, 91, 92, 93, 97, 112,
    119
Proudhon (Joseph-Pierre) 20, 33, 44,
    61, 135, 136, 153

Q

quasi-cause 114, 115, 117, 146

R

race 3, 19, 50, 51, 70, 72, 73, 131, 141,
    149, 155
races 155
racial 30, 49, 72, 145, 154, 155
racialization 70
racialized 75
racism 2, 8, 36, 143, 150
recursion 83, 118, 158
recursive 84, 88
recursivity 158
redundant 26
redundancies 52, 86
redundancy 86, 110, 111, 112,
    114, 119, 145
reflexive impotence 14, 92
refrain 108, 111
refrains 44
regime 14, 27, 34, 47, 64, 133
regularity 66, 87
regularities 116
rent 27, 46, 49, 50, 51, 53, 56, 59, 60,
    61, 74, 79, 131
represent 20

representation 16, 20, 26, 42, 48,
    65, 135, 145
representational 42
representations 108
representative 13, 36, 42, 43, 65,
    125, 149
represented 91, 142
represents 13, 52, 144
repress
    repressed 23, 69, 98
    repressing 30
    repression 22, 23, 24, 25, 27, 28,
        29, 66, 67, 68, 69, 74, 86, 99,
        127, 144
    repressive 22, 23, 23, 61, 69, 96,
        116, 137
    repressive-disciplining 67
resemblance 16
resonance 7, 21, 47, 48, 69, 70
    resonances 4, 115
    resonate 19, 21, 47, 52, 106, 110,
        117, 133
    resonated 3, 18
    resonates 40, 94, 96
retention 90, 91, 103, 119
    retentional 111, 114, 119
    retentions 90, 91, 92, 93, 112, 119
reterritorialize 131
    reterritorialization 131
    reterritorializations 142
    reterritorializing 131
reticulate
    reticulated 87, 92, 93, 103, 120
    reticulates 92
    reticulation 95
revolution 5, 71, 99, 105, 112, 120, 121,
    122, 124, 125, 126, 127, 129,
    130, 131, 133, 134, 135, 136,
    137, 138, 139, 140, 141, 142,
    143, 145, 147, 150, 154, 159
    révolution 134
    revolutionaries 154
    revolutionary 6, 8, 29, 31, 35, 76,
        108, 117, 122, 125, 127, 129,

    130, 131, 133, 134, 135, 136,
    138, 139, 140, 141, 142, 143,
    144, 145, 146, 150
revolutions 128, 136, 146
risk 7, 82, 83, 86, 87, 88, 134
    risks 115
ritornello 99, 108, 111
Rojava 54, 96, 97, 154

S
schizoanalysis 95, 99, 142, 143
segment 48, 52
    segmentalized 61
    segmentarity 29, 51, 52
    segmentation 50, 51
    segmented 51, 52
    segments 133
short-circuit 90, 109, 110
    short-circuited 81, 93, 98, 105,
        106, 118, 122
    short-circuiting 81, 103, 104, 119,
        150
    short-circuits 15, 93, 105, 120
sign 47, 94, 149, 150, 151, 152
    signed 128
    signs 22, 26, 47, 64, 73, 150
signal
    signalling 117
    signals 119
significance 112
significant 27, 58, 128, 157
    significance 19
    significantly 20
    signification 1, 47
    significations 26
signify
    signifier 47
    signifying 145
Silvia Federici 24
Simondon (Gilbert) 81, 91, 94, 109,
    116, 117, 120, 121
social 2, 4, 6, 7, 13, 14, 15, 18, 19, 20,
    23, 25, 28, 30, 31, 34, 37, 39,
    41, 44, 45, 46, 47, 48, 50, 51, 52,

53, 63, 64, 65, 67, 68, 70, 71, 72, 74, 75, 76, 77, 78, 79, 83, 84, 86, 88, 89, 92, 93, 95, 96, 97, 98, 101, 102, 103, 106, 108, 109, 125, 127, 133, 136, 137, 138, 140, 141, 143, 154, 156
social-ecological 96, 97
state 1, 3, 4, 5, 7, 11, 13, 14, 15, 17, 18, 19, 20, 24, 25, 26, 27, 28, 29, 30, 31, 32, 33, 35, 36, 37, 38, 39, 40, 41, 42, 43, 44, 45, 46, 47, 48, 49, 50, 51, 52, 53, 54, 55, 56, 59, 60, 61, 62, 63, 64, 65, 66, 67, 69, 70, 72, 73, 74, 75, 79, 87, 88, 96, 97, 98, 103, 109, 112, 113, 120, 121, 129, 130, 131, 132, 133, 134, 137, 138, 139, 140, 142, 143, 144, 145, 149, 150, 155, 156, 157, 159
  statist 4, 5, 6, 11, 13, 14, 15, 17, 19, 20, 21, 22, 23, 24, 25, 27, 29, 30, 31, 36, 37, 39, 40, 41, 42, 49, 74, 134, 135, 141, 153
Stiegler (Bernard) 6, 7, 76, 81, 83, 87, 88, 89, 90, 91, 92, 93, 94, 95, 96, 98, 99, 102, 103, 104, 105, 106, 114, 115, 119, 122, 133, 143, 151
stratify 48, 74
  stratification 7, 41, 50, 51, 53, 63, 65, 68, 70, 92, 131
  stratifications 131
  stratified 51, 55, 61
  stratifies 133
  stratifying 65
stratum 128
striate 74
  striated 25, 49, 55, 61
  striates 46, 53, 132, 133
  striating 131
  striation 50
subject 5, 68, 69, 86, 87, 90, 140, 151, 155

subject-group 144
subject-groups 144
subjugate 47
  subjugated 51, 134, 138, 144
  subjugated group 144
  subjugation 24, 36, 72
surplus labour 50, 54, 65, 80
surplus product 65
surveillance 7, 48, 78, 83, 84, 85, 88
symptom 22, 94, 103
  symptoms 9, 22, 94, 123, 136, 142
symptomatology 5, 22, 29, 29, 31, 36, 93, 94, 112, 136
  symptomatological 22
  symptomatologically 135

T
tax 25, 26, 45, 51, 55, 56, 57, 58, 59, 60, 61, 63, 74, 132
  taxable 55
  taxation 46, 49, 51, 52, 59, 60, 63, 79, 131
  tax-collecting 55
  taxed 33
  taxes 57, 61, 64
territorial 25, 26, 131
territorialize
  territorialized 49
  territorializing 15
throw of the dice 106, 119, 121, 152
trade 8, 34, 60, 61, 75, 82
  trading 62, 79
transgenerational memory 6, 25, 89
transindividualization 93
transindividuate
  transindividuated 91
  transindividuating 114
  transindividuation 91, 93, 95, 98, 103, 105, 106, 107, 109, 110, 114, 122, 123, 147, 150, 151, 158
  transindividuations 93
transindividuation 93

U
unthought 105
untimely 105, 108, 145
Urstaat 37, 40, 41, 130
utopia 113, 114, 115, 116, 118, 135
    utopian 8, 106, 113, 114, 117, 118,
        123
    utopianism 99, 113

V
valorize
    valorization 95, 98
    valorizes 65
vectoralist classes 85
vectors 85, 86
virtual 62, 99, 107, 109, 116, 117, 120,
    121, 141, 158
Voltairine de Cleyre 72

W
war machine 37, 40, 124, 129, 130,
    131, 132, 133, 134, 137, 138,
    146, 156
wound 103, 107, 119
    wounding 107
    wounds 117, 122

Y
yet-to-come 2, 8, 106, 113, 114, 116,
    117, 118, 122, 123

Z
Zapatismo 5, 140, 142, 144, 145
Zapatista 54, 108, 140, 141, 144
    Zapatistas 42, 54, 120, 122, 132,
        140, 143, 145, 147, 154